In Peace
Japan
Breeds War

BOOKS BY

GUSTAV ECKSTEIN

NOGUCHI

LIVES

KETTLE

HOKUSAI

CANARY

CHRISTMAS EVE

IN PEACE JAPAN BREEDS WAR

HARPER & BROTHERS
PUBLISHERS

IN PEACE JAPAN BREEDS WAR

By GUSTAV ECKSTEIN

HARPER & BROTHERS
NEW YORK AND LONDON

This book is complete and unabridged
in contents, and is manufactured in strict
conformity with Government regulations
for saving paper.

To

GODFREY KLINGER

Apr 45

TABLE OF CONTENTS

Introduction

I WENT TO JAPAN THE FIRST TIME ON AN IMPULSE. I was talking to a Japanese scientist who had worked in this country many years, and was my friend, when he had the sudden idea that I ought to go, and proved that he could make it possible in spite of my small purse, provided I went on a Japanese freighter, and provided I were willing to live like a poor but respectable Japanese. I set off. It was very exciting, especially as the freighter got further out along the Aleutians, and nearer the Japanese coast. My idea of Japan at the time could have been pretty much summed up in the two words, Far East. I pictured the Japanese as a tiny people, who drank tea, rode in the rikisha, produced Japanese prints, wood carvings, and silk, and spent much of their days and nights smiling and bowing.

It was the year of the American Exclusion Act. In fact, the freighter would put in on the very day the Act went into effect. To us in America the Act was simply a practical matter—we could not compete with a people whose standard of living was so low. We meant no offense. But in Japan there was burning national anger.

The freighter slowed down at dawn. I saw Fuji. I saw Yokohama. I saw a coolie on a sampan glance furtively toward the freighter, drop his pants, fall dead as a stone into the water, bathe, then dry himself by slipping into a kimono. I heard the first multitudinous sound of the wood clogs beating the earth. I smelled the land. Then, abruptly, all this sensuous satisfaction was chilled into an uneasiness. A little thing accounted for it. Doctors had arrived on board to meet me. They introduced me around, but failed to mention what country I came from, and one just coolly said I came from Germany. The uneasiness grew. It was never fully to leave me, not on subsequent visits either, and there were times when it would amount to fear. I tried to rationalize it. Partly it was the Exclusion Act—on that first day an unknown Japanese stole the American flag from the Embassy in Tokyo. Partly it was my timidity. Partly it was the shock of being thrust into a country so very different.

I recall the night I decided I would return to the United States sooner than I had planned. I was with one of the doctors in a wide-open second-story room of a small hotel. I did not want him to be pained. I told him what was true, that I wished to stay, that many people had been kind to me, that I had had more fleeting experiences of charm

than I ever had had in Europe, but that I was nervous.
I did not know exactly why, though the general unfriendly
feeling toward Americans was part of it, I thought. The
doctor argued with me. Then he lost patience. "If it is an
unannounced outbreak of war you are worried about, that
is silly. Countries do not go to war for sentimental reasons. They have real reasons. There are none such now
between the United States and Japan. And suppose there
were war! Do you think us uncivilized? You would not
be hurt. You would not be imprisoned. You would be
safe. You would be well fed. You would merely have to
stay in Japan a year or two. I think—yes, you would be
better off than in your own country."

I sailed. I remember the relief I felt as the land disappeared. There was no war. I decided I had been, as the
doctor implied, silly, and when the opportunity came to
return to Japan I snatched at it. I returned again and
again. The subsequent ventures were less upsetting than
the first, so I learned less. I had come in the meantime to
know a number of Japanese. I corresponded with several.
I read some of the history. I was more interested in Japan,
I suppose, than in any country but my own. I made a brief
plunge into the language, gave it up. The steady small
stream of Japanese business men and scientists that—to
our cost—was always entering at San Francisco and leaving at New York would sometimes pass through my city,
and one or another would come up to my laboratory and

look around. I made the acquaintance of an ambassador, a consul, a few Japanese-Americans in New York, a few on the west coast. I am myself a doctor. When Hideyo Noguchi, the bacteriologist of the Rockefeller Institute, died of yellow fever in West Africa where he was investigating it, I saw in that a subject that included both Japanese and medicine, so undertook to write his biography, and lived, as one does, for the next two years somewhere at the back of my subject's head. I visited his birthplace in the north of the main island, interviewed his sister, the tears of trachoma dripping from her gradually blinding eyes, interviewed his old teacher, saw the village, the castle, the waterfalls. After the book was published I was invited, indirectly by the Japanese Foreign Office, to return to Japan, but decided against going, because I suspected that I was somehow to be used for propaganda.

That is the total of my experience with the Japanese. I felt more and more that I understood them. I felt at home with them. I felt that certain of the things said about them were simply ignorance of them. Many were intelligent. Many were ambitious. Many were irritatingly aggressive. Some were gentle. Some were sensitive. But I never, I think I can truthfully say, believed that Japan was more than superficially a modern country. I believed that it was back in the fifteenth century, and that what it said in terms of the nineteenth was largely borrowed words. However, the fifteenth century had its strengths.

And Japan had those strengths. I always suspected that its present was spending, perhaps squandering, what its past had earned and saved. I suspected that if there were ever anything could give our country serious difficulty with Japan it would be qualities that came out of that old. That old is still everywhere just outside the cities, and in the cities lightly covered. It was increasingly plain from my first visit that there was a humor and a coarseness and a cruelty unimagined by Lafcadio Hearn. As I have said, I felt I understood them.

But I did not. Not deeply. Despite my experience, despite that I did not take the usual view that they were all deceit or all politeness, I know now that the nation seemed to me one thing and was another. I am amazed I could approach so close and still be so far. I am shaken by what has occurred. I am admittedly affected in all my judgments by recent events.

Since December 7th I have reconsidered everything. I have remembered the village where I lived with a Japanese family in their two-hundred-year-old house, have wondered what they were thinking. I have remembered the occasional eminent man I met, have wondered how he regarded the war. I have thought of the daily habits, the children, the small theaters, the nightly gossip, the prejudices. I have recalled the scraps of history told to me. And out of all that, this book. It is mainly a revisiting of scenes. A preponderant part has to do with the extreme south, and the south has had a large part in the nation's history. The Nipponese in Tokyo may smile sarcastically when he refers to some "eminence" down there—somewhat the feeling of all norths towards all souths—but he need not. The south has put him where he is. The book, then, is a travelogue, but a travelogue in which I frequently intrude to explain what I could not possibly at the time, what represents my greatly altered view.

There has been something accumulative in me in the course of the writing, a growing picture of the Japanese mind. I do not feel a great confidence in understanding that mind. But there has emerged the picture. I misunderstood it when I was near it, or misunderstood it partly. Today it has become something clearer, something more ominous, something that I ought to share.

In Peace
Japan
Breeds War

CHAPTER ONE
A First Night

THE PROVINCE OF SATSUMA IS THE SOUTHWEST CORNER of the most southerly of the four main islands. Its capital and principal city is Kagoshima. I arrived there on a July night. I was to be the guest of a surgeon. He called for me at the train, introduced me at his house, then went to see a patient. The portable partitions that would have divided the house into rooms had been taken away, so that it was all one great open space with a narrow veranda of polished pine around the edges. Beyond the house on three sides was a bamboo fence, and on the fourth side a miniature garden.

The surgeon's wife made me understand that I was to be at my ease—meaning I was not to try to squat Japanese fashion, but to sit with my legs extended out in front of me. I was placed so as to face the garden. She was near me, squatted rigidly. A son, thirteen years old, was also inside the room. But his two sisters, the one fifteen, the other seventeen, stayed off just where the room met

I

the veranda. The talk was quiet, and could be, for the hot city of Kagoshima lay noiselessly around. Very soon the moon rose, and though it was hidden by the garden wall, it lit a sky full of thin clouds. The boy was anxious to talk, the surgeon's wife said only an occasional word, the two girls said nothing. All knew a little English. Later, on the road outside we heard the sound of approaching *geta*, wood clogs, then a creaking of the bamboo garden door, then a stir in the vestibule. Then the husband was standing there, hatless, in white kimono, a shirt underneath. His hair was shorn smooth, making his head yet bigger, and his head making his body yet bigger. The bodies are apt to be big in Satsuma, big even in our sense. The husband entered the room not as the others had, on their knees, but strode in with heavy steps, and the floor swayed. He dropped to his knees. There followed the customary, prolonged, wholly stylized, greeting. Now I noticed that the women were out of the room—the two girls so far into the shadow that they could not be seen, the wife where, though still seen, she was definitely on the veranda. She wore a black kimono, had black hair and black eyes. She hereafter rarely entered the conversation. When her husband addressed her he did not turn his head her way, simply lowered his eyes a trifle, by a trifle bent his head, seemed to be looking at his feet. His broad back was squarely to her.

The talk turned to hunting. Thence went to dogs.

Thence to quail. Thence to the acumen of animals. Thence
to war and strategy. Thence to a Japanese hero, a former
citizen of the city, Saigo. I knew nothing of Saigo—the
surgeon could hardly believe it when I said so. He sketched
for me the history of Japan since the Revolution, left in
me the feeling that Saigo had done it all. He talked of
Saigo as if he had known him, and, of course, was too
young for that. He said several times that Saigo had re-
stored the Emperors to their former power. That is, the
Restoration had followed the Revolution. I suggested that
Saigo might be like Napoleon. The surgeon thought not.
He illustrated. He said that Saigo had once said: "My
profession is that of farmer." And that Saigo's lieutenant
had said: "I am the heavens and the universe." Napoleon,
he thought, was more like Saigo's lieutenant, Saigo perhaps more like Paul Krüger. The surgeon was thinking
now of the Rebellion that followed the Restoration—Saigo
rebelling against the Emperor whom he had helped to restore. What the surgeon meant about Paul Krüger was
that the Satsuma forces were small, like the Boer forces,
and the Emperor's forces drawn from a large nation, like
Great Britain. And he definitely called the Emperor's
forces, the forces of the *invader*. That was curious. This
was three-quarters of a century after the Rebellion, and
here was a citizen of Kagoshima still thinking of the forces
of the Emperor as the invaders of the territory of the
Lord of Satsuma. What made this yet more curious was

that the surgeon was educated at the University of Washington in America. Three years in America, a modern scientific medical practice, three-quarters of a century after the emergence of the new Japan—this Satsuman was still not quite a citizen of the Empire, and still somewhat a samurai of the Lord of Satsuma.

After a while the moon rose up over the garden wall, hunks of lava from a volcanic island out in Kagoshima Bay, casting long shadows. I could see also the shadows of the two girls. Presently the wife bowed. The two girl-shadows bowed. There were some mumblings of apology, and the three women were gone. The man-child remained. There was more talk of hunting and war. Then a small meal. Rice and fish and tea. In the midst of it, without any lead from the conversation, the surgeon said quietly that he wished his country would wipe off the insult, declare war on mine. I was amazed. I asked, "What insult?" He answered, "The insult of the Exclusion Act."

CHAPTER TWO
To Keep the Population Boiling

THE NEXT MORNING HE TOOK ME TO THE MUSEUM. WE passed two graveyards, one with the fallen of the Imperial Army, the other with the fallen of the Rebel Army. Those are dead that would not mix even today. The one graveyard had a disorderly individuality, the other a checkerboard neatness. In the first lay those who had fought on the side of the clan and against the Emperor, in the second those who had fought on the side of the Emperor, clan dead among the latter also. Seventy thousand died in the Rebellion. This Satsuma countryside was swept clean of men. Nothing remained but the cripples. Every house went in mourning, and the spirits were low, for the defeat was stinging, but the vitality of Satsuma was great and soon broke through, gave to the new Japan much of its physical strength, its passionate feelings, its bluster, its fanatic courage, all that makes it dangerous for the peace of the world. I walked in the clan graveyard. The youngest was fourteen—thirteen, as we figure it.

It began to rain a soft rain. A young skinny boy came hesitantly with an umbrella. He had all the while been keeping respectfully near. It had got around that the surgeon had a foreign visitor. The young skinny boy nervously opened the umbrella and held it up over me. He wore Western clothes. The surgeon ignored him, though he did mention that he was the son of a doctor. The boy held the umbrella so that I had all of it. I objected. No use. It was his chance to talk German to a foreigner. He said that he was studying German. Last year he had read *Minna von Barnhelm*, this year he was reading Grülpatzer. Next year he would be reading Schopenhauer. Then he would go to Tokyo to the Imperial University. Then he would go to Germany. After that he would be a philosopher. What the poor skinny boy could not foresee—what I later learned—was that in Tokyo he would marry a white girl. He would defiantly take her with him to Europe. And that would be the end. He would have used his frail flare of youth to break through a family tradition, and the flare would go right out. A skinny boy against the Japanese family. A mouse against a mountain.

We had gotten to the door of the Museum. The boy would like to have squeezed in with us. The surgeon gave him no opportunity, so he stood outside with his umbrella, hoped the rain would go on.

Specifically the Museum was to Saigo. In peace-time these Satsumans remember war. Tucked away in a small

Japanese house, the Museum did its part to keep history alive and the population boiling. In it were Saigo's belongings and the mementos of the Rebellion. Flags of the Satsuma Army. A spear. A *naginata*, which is a long-handled sword. Numerous other swords. Two military caps. Two military hats. Two belts. One Western-type uniform. A watch that Saigo had with him during the Rebellion. An iron kettle used and highly valued by him. Clogs that he made himself, and wore. His tobacco pouch. His plough. His wooden saddle. A kimono that his friend Gessho wore when he drowned. A kimono that Saigo wore when he tried to drown. Lanterns used by the clan army and by the army of the Emperor—they looked like bushel baskets. A farmer's door with bullet holes. A pistol given by Saigo to a young man as a wrestling prize. Many specimens of his handwriting. His writing brushes. His Chinese poems. A huge statue of him—he was bushy-browed, frog-eyed, wore a number nineteen collar, a head to match the neck, a body to match the head, generally suggested womb, men-children womb, soldiers. Then, a succession of photographs of his disciples, many of the great of the nation, names that stand out in the Revolution, the Restoration, the Rebellion, in the Sino-Japanese War, in the Russo-Japanese War, even in the background of World War I, and it would be interesting to know their prowess, doubtless considerable, in World War II. Okubo, Admiral Togo, Kuroki, Kawakami, Kabayama, Oyama, Yamamoto, Mori, Matsukawa, Oura, Taziri, Saigo the younger.

And finally, among all the Japanese objects, suddenly a violently contrasting photograph, signed. *To the Museum of the Hero of Kagoshima, with profound admiration—Mussolini.* It was a photograph of the early Mussolini, soon after the march on Rome, worlds to conquer, but none of the brutality of conquering, before Ethiopia, before Hitler, before the invasion of Manchuria. He was large-bodied but not fat, a lightness even in the static photograph.

We came out of the Museum. There was the young skinny boy with the umbrella. But now it did not rain. He kept walking behind us.

CHAPTER THREE
Takamori Saigo Samurai

THE SURGEON HAD THOUGHT SAIGO WAS NOT LIKE Napoleon. I thought he was. Not so fast a mind, not so large a world, East not West, not such brilliant battles, but the same simple origin, each rising to Commander-in-Chief of the forces of his nation, each inspiring fanatic loyalty, then the sudden decline, the retirement from public life, the meteoric reappearance, the quick rallying of all the old followers, but on a dying stage, then the end—Saigo's that of an antique Roman, Napoleon's a lingering cancer at St. Helena. And after each was dead there was a legend.

Saigo was born in 1827. His father was a samurai—wore the two swords, the long one to dispose of the enemy, the short one to dispose of himself should he ever fall into dishonor.

The son belted on the two swords at twelve, which was the law, and about that law he was punctilious. The following year he fought a duel, was wounded so as to be permanently handicapped for any expertness at swords. He studied hard. His progress was slow but stubborn. His stepmother saw what he was—saw through the giant bulk and had the highest expectations. To help him keep at his schoolwork she would have his sister stay in the room with him, and if he fell asleep, it was the sister who was punished. Sometimes he studied with the Zen priest. The priest would put a question to him. He would squat on a stone and grope his way to the answer. *Question:* There is that heavy temple column over there—how would you bring it three feet closer? *Answer:* Move myself three feet nearer. *Question:* A pearl is at the bottom of the sea. How would you get it without wetting your hand? *Answer:* If it is not worth wetting your hand, it is not worth getting. *Question:* What is it drops up instead of down? *Answer:* The reflection of the wistaria.

There were eighty-four provinces in that old Japan. The number of provinces in any one clan varied. The provinces had their lords, the clan had its lord, and both had their samurai to defend them. The most powerful clan for more than two hundred years was that at Yedo. The Lord of Yedo was the Shogun, technically the Emperor's military leader, actually the ruler of the country. But the Shogun's power had long been declining, and since the south was far from Yedo, the declining was quickest there. The Lord of Satsuma lived haughtily in Kagoshima. The Shogun lived in Yedo. The Emperor lived in Kyoto. The Shogun operated by a complicated system of checks. In every province and in every clan he had his spies. Lord was set in watch over lord. The clans were kept financially weak, so even should they wish to rise they would lack the materials of war. Each lord had an estate in Yedo, was required to live there up to half of the year, or every alternate year, and to have his family there the rest of the time, these thus hostages. The pilgrimage from Satsuma to Yedo—from the extreme south to about the middle of the islands—was in consequence a regular affair. It was long, arduous, and through every kind of country. In 1853 there was a special calling of the clans, and this was Saigo's opportunity. He was appointed to the retinue. On the way the Lord of Satsuma fell into talk with him, was struck by his intelligence, by the unusual mingling of hot samurai youth and inborn human wisdom. So as to continue the talks in Yedo, and still not make too conspicuous that a lord was having so much to do with his servant, the Lord appointed Saigo his gardener. The maid reports that she knew whenever Saigo was the visitor, because the Lord would empty his pipe so often, knock it so excitedly on the tobacco *bon*.

The clans met. The clans plotted. The clans scattered. Saigo stayed on in Yedo as gardener. Murder and counter-murder were in the air, and the whole Japanese world was at it, which naturally made the gardener's position not altogether pastoral. He disappeared from Yedo. He reappeared in Kyoto, the Emperor's city.

In Kyoto there was the chief priest, Gessho. Gessho also was in the plot to overthrow the Shogun, so the men of the Shogun were after him. Saigo appointed himself Gessho's bodyguard. Strange brotherhood. Something vaguely feminine about both their immensities. Together they fled from Kyoto, made their way cautiously to Satsuma, and there the new young Lord, for the old had died, respectfully suggested they give themselves up to Yedo— for execution. Instead they packed a Chinese sampan with a banquet, pushed out to sea, filled themselves with food, toasted each other in rice wine, wrote each a Chinese poem which he attached to his body, then plunged overboard into the ocean. You almost think you can hear the splash, those two hulks, those two patriots, gorged with food, paddled on their backsides by the waves, the poems tied to them like express tickets. A samurai and a priest. The priest drowned. The samurai floated. Loyal friends on the shore—and Saigo had by now a growing gang—were suspicious of the actions of the two brothers, so searched the sea and found Saigo's half-drowned body.

Saigo was banished to Oshima. He had been banished to Oshima before, for poaching. He was beginning to know Oshima. He would be banished there again. On one of the banishments the magistrate so admired him that he gave him his daughter to sleep with. On another banishment, however, Saigo was stuck into a cage so small

he was never able to stand straight up, and was kept in
the cage so long that when Satsuma sent for him, because once more in trouble, he was so lame he had to be
supported by two men as he walked, and in that condition
had to roll in a small boat for fourteen days. But perhaps
he did not mind. His loyalty was such that on several
similar occasions he was known to say: "If the Lord wants
it so, so it must be."

By 1866 the Revolution finally got under way. A prince
of the blood was the commander of the Imperial troops,
but that was nominal. The actual commander was Saigo.
The Imperial troops scored an initial victory near Kyoto.
They pushed on toward Yedo. When they were within
seventeen miles—as the story was told me in Kagoshima
—Saigo went on alone. Walked. He met there with the
envoy of the Shogun. The two entered a tent. Many
hours elapsed. Finally, a follower of Saigo, suspecting
murder, stole up to the tent, peeped through a hole, and
there were the two playing chess. The surrender of the
future Tokyo had been bloodlessly attained. The envoy
had immediately agreed to the surrender. Saigo wanted
proof. The envoy said that the castle would be turned
over the next day. Saigo could not see why, since it was
to be the next day, it could not be that night. What reason to wait? It was turned over that night.

There were still battles. One was at Aizu, in the north,
where Hideyo Noguchi, the bacteriologist, was born. His

mother had a hand in that. Terrible battles. Fathers dying, sons dying, mothers killing their own babies rather than having them captured. History says that the Imperial troops were too ruthless. But it was civil war, and most countries sooner or later learn what that means, and civil war in Japan would have an especially mediaeval quality.

In consequence of all this the clans became a united Empire. The new Japan. A surge of patriotism swept them. Each wanted to give something, gave, was urged to give more, suddenly found itself sliding faster than it had meant to, and presently there were no clans left. The estates of the lords were gone. The clan armies were merged into the national army. And natural that Saigo should be Commander-in-Chief of this new national army. Still something upside-down about it—a samurai leading orderly mechanized troops. Drill, drill, drill. No temperament. No brawls. An army of commoners. The whole thing disgusted him. Furthermore, he did not like Tokyo, did not like the new government, did not like the men who were around the Emperor. The new laws outraged him. The samurai class to be abolished! Soldiers no longer to do up their hair! It to be illegal to belt on the two swords!

He demanded action for his army. The new government allowed him an expedition against the headhunters in Formosa. That was not very amusing. What he really wanted was to invade Korea. An old idea with him. He had drawn plans years before. He knew just how he would do it. And was there not justification! Were not the Koreans insolent! The new government had sent representatives to make a treaty, and the Koreans had rejected them. As a matter of fact, the Koreans seemed to have no clear idea whom the representatives represented. The very British legation on the spot in Yokohama had some trouble keeping clear just whom the representatives represented, or just what "Emperor" meant, or what "Shogun" meant. Saigo was denied his invasion. The new government decided that it wanted first to have time to get itself firm within—chances enough later for conquest abroad. Had Saigo been a ruffian he would now have acted on his own authority. But individual ruthlessness was not his role. He was a samurai with something akin to chivalry in him.

He resigned. He went back to Satsuma. His followers wanted to go back with him. He would not hear of it. Satsuma blood must strengthen the new Empire. Satsuma men must fill the influential places. Perhaps, also, he foresaw that there was going to be trouble in Satsuma. He did not want the best wiped out by whatever might happen.

Outside the city he had his cave. He wrote poetry. He played the lute. He farmed a piece of land. He meditated. As of old he disciplined himself answering Zen-priest questions. Every now and then here or there in the province he started a school—a hotbed. It was a fresh generation listening to him now, but it had the old generation's blood in its veins. If the Emperor in Tokyo was surrounded by weakening influences something ought to be done. If the new government was effeminate the whole country would soften and rot. Rebellion! It has been said that Saigo had nothing to do originally with the Rebellion, that the pupils simply had taken possession of the master—an old trick, removing blame from rulers by laying it on subordinates. In Tokyo they were saying that the young officers down there in the south were forcing Saigo's hand. Satsumans claim even now that Saigo was out hunting when he heard that the clan was on the march. Possibly. And anyway, once the clan was on the march, there was nothing for Saigo to do but to lead it. So, this time, he was leading an army not for the Emperor, but against the Emperor. And this army was not the newfangled Western type. This army was still to use its swords.

Okubo, head of the new government, was also a Satsuman, a clansman of Saigo. In him there was no division of loyalty. First he tried the simpler way—assassination. He sent nineteen young men down to Satsuma, to find Saigo and murder him. The nineteen were discovered. The facts were placarded over the countryside. Satsuma was in a rage. Nothing could have stopped the Satsuman army now. Okubo had Saigo outlawed by Imperial edict, and the new army started south. Saigo's own brother was in it. The large significance of this movement south Tokyo clearly saw. It would be the trial and the proof. It would

show whether the new Japan was strong enough to quell
uprisings within its own confines. It was the test at home
for what later might be risked abroad. The Tokyo newspapers said that the flesh ought to be eaten off Saigo's
bones, that his treason was supernatural. Nevertheless the
commander of the new army sent word on ahead to Saigo,
assured him that the new army was aware it was moving
against its teacher and friend, but that it was defending
the Emperor, and that Saigo would understand. And he
did. It was never a question with him of Saigo against the
Emperor—that is fairly unthinkable in Japan no matter
how hypocritical the set-ups sometimes look from without. It was Saigo against the "bad advisors" around the
Emperor.

For Saigo it was the end. It was not only guns against
swords, but new against old, collectivism against inspired
individualism, the world against Satsuma. It was the twilight of the samurai. It was the dawn of the commoner.
The odds were too great. Saigo was wounded. He with-
drew from the field. He called his lieutenant, asked the
lieutenant to behead him. The lieutenant shrank. Saigo's
wrath rose—would the lieutenant prefer that a private perform the task? The lieutenant unsheathed his sword. Saigo
thanked him. Saigo bent his massive head. Off it went.
The work done the lieutenant committed suicide, died next
his chief. The lieutenant was twenty-three. And thus ended
the Rebellion—they pronounce the word gloomily to this

hour in Kagoshima. Saigo is alive to this hour in Kagoshima. Not a day but the Kagoshima newspaper remembers some anecdote. Not a day but the teacher mentions
him to her class. The bloody head the Satsuma troops
quickly hid in a strawstack. But the Imperial troops
searched—were not going to let their victory go un-
crowned. One of Saigo's own old pupils received the head,
washed it, gave it burial.

CHAPTER FOUR
If One Has the Opportunity to Travel

Kagoshima lies on a bay of the same name well above where it narrows into the China Sea, about sixty miles by train. Near there is Port of Bo. It was arranged I go to Port of Bo to fish. I rode in a second-class coupé. The train waited a time in Kagoshima Station. Suddenly the door of the coupé flew open and two army officers lunged in. The first was moustached, cravenetted, booted, sworded. He looked rough. He dropped into his seat, passed his hand over his insignia, let that introduce him. I tried a word of English. He groaned. I tried German. He groaned again. But at the first French phrase, up he leapt, brightened, said he had not spoken French for a generation, nevertheless we would get on extravagantly. From his pocket he brought some tissue-thin Japanese paper and a pencil, and we embarked on a bastard communication, part written, part talk, part gesture, all clear, the conscience for syntax easy on both sides.

"Six children I have," he explained, "and a seventh

is—how do they say?—no matter. The oldest, sixteen, has
his heart on engines. I would rather it were on campaigns.
Studies night and day, till I am afraid of the student's
disease." He punched his chest significantly. The thought
was unpleasant. He was absent-minded a moment, then
turned, tapped his finger near the medallion on the coat
of his superior. His superior possibly expected some logic
in the tap, possibly resented the familiarity, said nothing.
The father turned again to me. "You like Japan? I refer
to the south, not the north. Satsuma. Near here is where
the race began. They were big, like me, not warts like the
men of the north. They came from the islands south of
here, swung their boats into the warm Japan current and
rode along with it. The point where they landed is well-
known. You must go there. It would interest you. My
oldest daughter is so very interested."

He realized I was an American. I was sure because
he did not ask. His mind was fairly made up about
Americans. Suddenly he said that he was very good at
jujitsu. He waxed enthusiastic. He stood up. He showed
how you hit not with the fist, but with the side of the hand.
He explained to me that the principle of jujitsu is to win
not by meeting strength with strength, but to win by giving
way before strength—giving way so that your adversary's
strength is used against itself. Your adversary drives at
you, and you yield, and he goes headlong. Or, if he has
bigger muscles, you drop back, then strike him suddenly,

from the side, from behind, or again and again and again,
and especially press at a point where he is acutely vulnerable. Best, too, if all this proceeds in complete silence. I
realized something about jujitsu—the Japanese not having
large bodies, but being contemptuous, and also ambitious,
must by an inevitable evolution come on a way of defense
and offense that compensated for their lack. Their pride
brought them to jujitsu. And by continuous training in it
they have doubtless made their minds even more the way
nature made them, shrewd and indirect. For your examination in jujitsu, he said, you were told to walk along a road,
someone without warning grabbed you from behind, and
if your defense was not instant and correct, with no
moment of surprise, you did not get your diploma. Or
you walked where there was a sheer drop, someone shoved
you off, and if you were hurt you did not get your diploma.

Then he was suddenly on another subject. "I must be
lazier than other men," he was saying. "Or why do I
not understand English? We have opportunity enough.
It is impossible to learn English in the schools, but there
are the Christian churches and the missionary clubs—if
you do not mind going to them. For myself, I choose to
be ignorant. Language makes no difference anyhow. It is
what is here." He indicated his heart as before he indicated
his lungs. "I have always had great interest in English-
speaking people. A military education requires French or
German. The books on tactics. . . ." He broke off. "My

country was with yours in the Great War. But the sympathy of the Army was divided. You think us a military nation. Like Germany. Like Russia. No. That is not true. . . ." He broke off again. "You do not want war, we do not want war, no one wants war." He lingered on that estimable opinion, glanced toward his superior, added perfunctorily, "except where the national honor is involved." The superior got deliberately up, deliberately walked to the other side of the coupé, gazed out over the dunes. The color of the sea and the lay of the land were like the Italian Riviera. We were all three now standing at the window. I told them that this part of the China Sea was like the Italian Riviera. "Ah, Italy, that is another beautiful country, that is like Satsuma," said the father. Then he added that one must learn more geography in a week of travel than in ten years of school.

And instantly the superior crashed in. "Yes, if one has the opportunity to travel! The citizens of some countries have the opportunity to travel! The citizens of some countries do not!" The train had eased into a station. The father saluted, bowed, smiled reassuringly, hurried off. The superior tramped after.

CHAPTER FIVE
I Understood the Fisherman

I T WAS EVENING WHEN I ARRIVED AT PORT OF BO. STILL an ancient place. Through Port of Bo came the earliest Chinese commerce. I slept the night in a small hotel. Not long after dawn a committee of the village came to take me to a locally important temple. Port of Bo lies on the side of a huge rock, the temple on the peak of the rock, the bay below the rock, beyond the bay the sea, and down from the temple a long broad precipitate approach of steps ending in a road that weaves its way through the town. As I descended the steps the townspeople filled in behind me to take a look at me. Wherever I came near them they began reflexly to bow, but if they could help it they did not let me come near, so that as I looked back, the populace was thinned close by, compact further on. The women and the girl-children were in kimono. The men, mostly fishermen and workers in the fisheries, were in the customary short pants and coat, but a few in loin cloths. The committee all was in dress kimono. The school-boys and schoolgirls wore the school uniforms.

The English teacher ran ahead of me, then got behind me, then hurried nervously ahead again, like a small dog. He was giving himself things to do. He was desperately responsible for me. He was telling everybody what not to do. He wore an American-type straw hat, a shabby cream-colored summer suit, shoes, and carried a cane. He spoke English, but I neither understood him nor did he understand me.

Finally we got down to a small wharf. There stood the fisherman. He smiled broadly to me—he did not bow—raised his hand in a loose welcome. The scant clothes that he had on him were practically off him, a thin cotton kimono that was really only a sail blowing in the wind, and a loin cloth. His body had striking solidity, one of the most beautiful bodies I had ever seen, more like something that had been poured instead of grown, tremendously relaxed, not yellow but a bronze-black. He was like nothing around, not taller, and not especially bigger, but knit in an entirely different way. He was startling. And it was startling also that there should be this type of Japanese. He and the little yellow salesman who hustles about the world can hardly be considered the same race.

The boat was there. It had a straw-matted floor. I slipped off my shoes. The fisherman took them, put them at one end in a parallel row with his own two straw sandals. Presently the shabby shoes of the English teacher were added to the row. I dropped into the boat in my stocking feet. The English teacher hurried in after. He was apparently to be the interpreter.

The boat had a mast but the sail was down. The bronze-black fisherman lightly slipped between us, began to maneuver a stern oar. We made a very decent pace. The bay, which the fisherman indicated was deep, was rimmed with a wall of rock, a natural breakwater, really the crest of a small range of hills. It was low tide. At high tide we would have been able to ride out to sea at a number of points, but at low tide there was only one narrow passage, sheer stone on either side, and stone below the water also, and not very far below, so that it was necessary to wait on a swell to carry the boat through. This maneuvering was extraordinary to see. The water of the bay was quiet except for the rhythm of the swells. The boat swiftly approached the passage, stopped almost dead, waited, lunged forward with the rising water, shot between the walls, was out to sea. The water was immediately restless like the sea.

The fisherman was now even more at home. He poured out a stream of talk, used his free hand to punctuate. The thin voice of the English teacher broke in to tell me what the fisherman said. I understood the fisherman but I did not understand the English teacher. I was sorry for the

little man. For a while I kept up pretending. But the flow
of the fisherman's talk was such that I was helplessly
caught in it. He was pointing to sky, to clouds, to objects
along the shore, to birds, to the surface of the sea, to
things within the sea. His kimono had dropped from him.
What we say at such a moment is "he stood there like a
God." But he did not at all, had none of that merely
anatomic character, but was a ceaselessly functioning, altogether human, perfectly adjusted machine. I think I got
the sense of everything he said.

Suddenly my attention was jerked back to the English
teacher. His American straw hat—with which he had been
having trouble all morning—would not stay on his Japanese head, and this time it skipped off into the water.
Left hand on the oar, right hand in the water, the fisherman gracefully returned it to him. Sad. From this on the
poor little man ceased to attempt to interpret. He was,
of course, the only English teacher in this whole neighborhood, had studied the language, no doubt, with another
who came before and who was like him. I would at that
moment have given a great deal to have understood his
speech. I was certainly in no frame of mind to make fun
of his difficulty. His linguistic catastrophe had pushed
him into a very low state indeed. He kept rubbing the
straw hat with his sleeve, which at least let him concentrate
on something that had nothing to do with conversation.
I could see it all. I could see exactly what had led up to

this instant. The mayor had had a letter that I was coming. A small ultra-formal, ultra-Japanese committee was appointed to set the stage for my arrival. The English teacher was of course the pillar of the committee. And he thought he would be, too, on this momentous morning. If he had doubts as to the limitations of his English, he had the warming reassurance of being the only one at the southern tip of Satsuma who knew any at all. Furthermore, he had been teaching it—he was a man of forty—at least twenty years, and after all that rehearsal, he was to have this day the opportunity of a public performance. I thought of the literate Japanese Empire—100,000,000 of them, as they claim—most of them sooner or later supposed to study some English, most of them subjected to the pathetic pedagogy that a man like this could give them, most of them getting a false confidence about understanding us through our language; and I had waked in me an additional awareness of the joint problem, theirs and ours, in the present and in the future. I was struck as never before in my life by what constitutes language. Only comprehension, which is based always ultimately on imagination, brings even wild and domestic animals into a mutually livable world with us. Language, on the contrary, so frequently tricks us as to one another. It gets in the way. It freezes our imagination. It is a first step in hostility. It often actually blocks communication between man and man.

The fisherman talked and oared. He had such energy! He was keeping parallel to the natural breakwater. It was anything but a stormy day, yet the small boat rolled frivolously. It could be imagined that the English teacher was getting seasick. I have almost never seen a Japanese seasick except in trans-Pacific steerages. This one at least was turning very pale. As we skirted near a point of land, he said something to the boatman, who angled the craft up close to the shore, and the English teacher, bowing many times to me, behaving utterly as if this had from the beginning been the plan, and no doubt with an enormous weight off him, almost leapt ashore. Without once looking back he hurried away across the sand.

CHAPTER SIX
Disciplined to the Sea

IMMEDIATELY THE FISHERMAN SWUNG THE BOAT around and made for an island that lay like one more wave on the surface of the water. The wind was rising— not a blow, just life come in it. He hoisted the sail. He fastened the ropes. He kept the prow on a steady line. His movements were as easy as a cat's. And as concentrated. He handled the boat as if it were one more limb of his body, as an American boy handles a Ford. In fact, the Japanese talent for the sea is as developed as the American for machinery. The sea is so all-present. The edges are everywhere matted with craft. A great part of the nation has something to do with small boats, manages them well, and that is at least a natural beginning for large boats. In late years the Japanese carried more and more, all that was possible of their cargoes in their own bottoms—further training. And one reason that we were never sure how much of the materials of war they were amassing.

29

When we got near to the island, perhaps a hundred yards, the fisherman threw out an anchor. He gave me a box that had a handle, and at the bottom side of it, a glass window. I might with that follow his movements as he fished—shove the box well into the water and look through the window. Spear fishing. He examined the spears that were sticks of bamboo sharpened at one end. His loin cloth dropped off him like an uninteresting thought. He slid into the water.

What ensued was the first fishing that has ever seemed to me even half-fair sport.

He had anchored the boat over what amounted to a submarine bay that I could see into easily because the water was clear and the sun shining. He took a deep breath—had lungs like the rest of us, but from the length of time he stayed under, you thought he must have gills. And he seemed not to be swimming like a human swimmer —used his arms and his legs less, and the musculature of his body more, its sinuous movement propelling it against the resisting water. He had a spear in each hand. He watched the fish as they passed him, let one after another go as not worth the chase. Then he saw one that pleased him. And the fish saw him, changed its direction. He changed his, flanked its movement. The fish promptly realized its peril. The fight for its life was on. It tried to head out to sea. The fisherman blocked the way. He swam exactly like the fish, there was no doubt. The fight gained in excitement. The fish began to be confused, and then, of course, was lost, for the man was not confused. He selected the stony corner that he thought best, kept now to either side of the tail of the fish, suddenly lunged, drove his spear into the fish and pinioned it against the stone. Then up he rose, dropped the wet wiggling creature into the end of the boat, careful not to get any sea water on his *tatami* or on my shoes, grinned to me, told me the kind of fish, took a deep breath, slid down in. Soon the back of the boat was full of the tormented life.

Then he came up once more, vaulted lightly into the boat, lifted the anchor, went to a new place, dropped the anchor, slid down into the water, looked about busily, came up, changed the position of the boat again, slid down in again. And this time he found what he was after. He signaled to me, wide open eyes, pointed. It took me some time to be sure I saw. An octopus.

He said it was a small octopus. I measured it afterward, a circumference of almost twelve feet, with the tentacles outstretched. Where we saw it first was on a rock on the bottom of the sea. He came up, got a knife with a blade of about eight inches. Then he dove down, swam around over the top of the octopus, carefully, I think—suddenly stabbed it through its hub, its vital center, its nervous system, seat of its personality, earthly repository of its spirit. It looked practically the same after the stab, the wave-like motions passed out over the tentacles, the body continued slowly to advance, and especially the suckers along the tentacles continued to suck, but the total powers were weakened. It was a tedious task to disengage those tentacles from the bottom of the sea. He got me to help, gave me a fistful of chains, at the one end of each chain a hook, and he would slip the hook under a tentacle, disengage it, and I would keep the chain taut to prevent the tentacle from again attaching itself. After about an hour the massive glistening thing, dead, dying, or very alive, depending upon how you thought of it, at once formed and formless, lay at the end of the boat among the fish, its suckers still functioning, still singly advancing, but co-ordination gone. The fisherman measured his catch with his eye. He said it was enough.

It was midday, time to eat. I wondered where. He pointed over toward the island. I thought he would row over. He shook his head. I offered to swim. He roared. Well, then? He indicated that he would carry me over. That seemed impossible. He assured me it was utterly possible. I started to take off my kimono. He wrapped it closer about me. And what he now did is incredible to me still, held me up over the water, carried me to the sand, set me down there in a state of mind somewhere between shame and dry respect. The sense of my helplessness comes back to me to this day. He dealt with the sea like a master. He and his ancestors and their ancestors had ceaselessly disciplined themselves to it.

Even on a modern trans-Pacific Japanese liner I once felt that inherited discipline. It was a September crossing, rough all the way, then suddenly the sea quieted, or perhaps we were just getting used to the motion. It was the night before the arrival at Yokohama—the captain's dinner, with confetti, horns, paper hats, like any transAtlantic liner. Toward the end of the dinner the captain rose to make, as we thought, a *sayonara* address. He did not. He merely said: "The ship will enter the typhoon at eleven o'clock tonight." And sat down. The party dampened considerably. It was the flatness of the statement. He had not said the typhoon would upset the ship, and he had not said the typhoon was nothing to worry about, but just coldly announced the time we would enter it. And we did enter it at eleven with an abruptness and exactness that made it seem as if the devil had arranged with the captain. We were none of us any the worse for the next eight hours, and you expect people of the sea to be used to the sea, but the casualness of that captain and that crew and the Japanese passengers against the poorly-concealed unrest of us Westerners was another concentrated bit of evidence of the way that nation has been disciplined to the sea. On the return trip of the same voyage there was a "good-weather" captain, fat as the wine god, began drinking, got drunk, insisted on wrestling on deck with a Buddhist priest and two passengers, threw all three. His face grew so red I expected him to have a heart attack. So a Japanese officer can be undisciplined, though he was the most undisciplined I have ever seen.

The fisherman grinned close into my face—had set me down on the sand as dry as a peanut. I think his stunt pleased even him. But he did not waste time over his pleasure. He swam several times out to the boat and back again, brought boiled rice, the live fish, tea, cooking utensils, chinaware, a knife that looked like a scimitar, went back and forth between boat and island like a cook between pantry and kitchen. On the sand he built a fire. He brewed the tea. He selected a smooth rock, laid one of the fish on it, and as fast as a machine slices bread, sliced fish, and the total creature kept its form as a loaf of bread may. He asked me whether I wanted my fish broiled, and broiled it. His he ate raw. There is some relation between raw fish—the eating of raw flesh generally—and a raw way of living. I have no idea what the physiology is. I suppose, however, that the Japanese would say that the underlying reason for their taste is that raw fish requires no heat, no charcoal, is more economical, and I suppose more healthful—provided you know fish. And the Japanese know fish. Somewhere near to a hundred million of them are living on fish flesh. Before the war fish was one of Japan's largest exports, canned salmon, crab, tuna. You see in their waters every variety of fishing—not much of it for amusement. The country has always been in some international fishery dispute. The Japa-

nese used to fish in our Alaskan waters—and measure
depths. Since 1937 they have not—some were shot at and
killed by our coast guards. Their fishing in Siberian waters
has, as everyone who reads the newspapers knows, been
the source of endless threat, negotiation, and agreement
with Russia. Part of the protest has been that the Japanese
have drained the sea, especially of salmon, by short-sighted
fishing methods.

My fisherman's appetite was enormous. He ate four
fish himself, which must have been five times as much
as I ate. He ate six bowls of rice. The townspeople had
sent along *Kirin* beer for me, and though the fisherman
guyed me with a grin, did not mind that I did not drink.
He finished off everything. And after lunch he did not
sleep. He walked all over the island. He looked before and
after and under everything, as if everything might have
a treasure value. Each time he picked up a pebble it would
be with an excited interest, and then would drop it dead.
He seemed even to have a savage curiosity about the tex-
ture of the sand, would take up handfuls and run his
thumb everywhere through it. We stayed about four hours,
and then he ate again, and then we started back the way we
came. The townspeople spied us long before I spied them.
There was a great crowd down at the wharf. The English
teacher was not there, but just before I entered the small
hotel a woman came, said in an English that I could almost
understand that she was the English teacher's sister, and

apologized for him—he had to go away, very urgent, a call to the next village. Poor little man. The fisherman did not follow with the crowd up into the town, but stood broadly on the wharf, filled the air with noises, made practically an oration of his *sayonara*.

CHAPTER SEVEN
They Are Slow at Some Things

I WANTED TO PAY MY BILL AT THE SMALL HOTEL. I indicated that I wanted to pay it. The host understood. The host left the room. He came back. He indicated that he protested to my paying the bill at all. I indicated that I must. He indicated that he had no idea how much it was. There was the charge for the room. There was the charge for renting the bedding. There was the charge for the charcoal. There was the charge for the tea. There was the charge for the hot bath. But, I indicated, how much was the total? He shook his head as if he did not know. He bowed. He left the room. He returned. He still protested. He still did not know. I insisted. He left the room. He returned with the bill carefully folded in an envelope, the envelope on a plate, and the plate covered and on a tray. He slid the tray toward me, and in the very act of sliding was still protesting. He left the room. I read my bill. There was also a heap of empty envelopes on the tray. I put the money for the bill into one of them, the tips for six serv-

37

ants, each separate, into the remaining—the number that had been brought was exactly seven—and pushed the tray in the general direction my host would return. I had been carefully instructed by the surgeon in Kagoshima that that was the way I must do it. After a long interval my host did return. He bowed. He behaved as if he did not see that the tray was there. Nevertheless he presently drew the tray after him out of the room. I wondered if I could go now. I had a feeling that I could not. So I stayed. The feeling was right. My host reappeared in the room, bowed sunnily, which meant that he was satisfied with the money, pushed the tray ahead of him, and on it was a gift from him and from each of the servants whom I had tipped. We bowed a good deal back and forth. I left the hotel. The host, his wife, his six servants followed me to the door.

As the surgeon in Kagoshima, who had been in America, impatiently expressed it: "If they only would speak out like business men! If they only would say what the price is and be done! But they never do! They never will! If a Japanese has been educated in America he fails in Japan—and the reason is, America has made him too direct." With a sigh he turned over on his bedding on the straw-matted floor and fell asleep.

CHAPTER EIGHT
The Young Man Saw His Task

ON THE TRAIN BACK—I WAS GOING VIA KAGOSHIMA to the village of Funakura—I met a Catholic priest, talked to him of Saigo, and he added the following story.

It was a rainy night. Saigo had called a rikisha. The runner was a delicate boy, and Saigo apologized that he should be pulled along in that manner. Was he not too heavy? The boy said no. Saigo watched the boy. How did it happen that one so young and delicate and with so intelligent a face should be a rikisha man? Saigo asked him. The boy assured him there was no hardship in this, quite the contrary, for he was earning his education. He went on to tell of his hopes. At the destination the young man helped the older down to the street. The older disappeared into the rain. The younger looked into his hand and found twenty *yen*! Who was this man? The boy thought back over all the quiet wise things his passenger had said.

Years passed. The Revolution was over. The younger once more met the older. Now he knew who the man was.

39

He knew too how he had profited by that rainy night. He owed everything to it. Years again. The Rebellion was over. Okubo was directly responsible for Saigo's death, and the young man clearly saw his task. It was a spring morning. In a picturesque dell two men with flowers in their hands were standing by the roadside. There were four in the shrubbery behind them. Okubo was being driven by his coachman to the palace. The coach was stopped, the horses mutilated, the coachman killed, then Okubo was run through with a sword. Okubo was reading his newspaper. "Ah," he said, "a moment yet, till I have read this to the end." And still reading, he died.

CHAPTER NINE
Silent Soldier

To KAGOSHIMA IT WAS SIXTY MILES, TO SENDAI thirty-eight more, and from Sendai five miles on foot to a single narrow street—the village of Funakura. There I was to live for the next three weeks. A delegation from the village came halfway to Sendai to meet me. Just as we were to step into the single street—it was three o'clock of a hot afternoon—there was a wild high cry. A human cry. Then the cry was repeated, but no one seemed to notice it. Then, however, one man noticed me. He was the doctor, and interpreter. He explained. "The insane man. Lives in that house on the other side of the rice field, alone with his wife. Sometimes makes that noise all day, sometimes all night. Sometimes runs after the children, but they do not pay any attention to him. Sometimes goes from house to house, announces old news—tomorrow will be telling everyone that you are coming." Was there no asylum, I asked. "There is the jail—if a man is insane enough. But why put him in the jail—if he can scream and run he is happy." I saw that jail, a small cold room.

I looked again at the gentlemen around me, each in his dress kimono, black silk, stiff and jutting. No one could have guessed that there were flexible bodies inside.

We reached the house I was to live in. It had a thatched roof two feet thick, so low that you needed to bend to get under it. The house was old—had been repaired and repaired till perhaps no part of the original remained—two hundred years old, they said. It sprawled about because it had grown as the family grew, built for bodies that never sat on chairs, rarely stood, commonly shuffled on their haunches. A whole civilization on its heels or knees, sliding, slipping, crawling, creeping. The mayor was the tallest man in Funakura. The mayor went ahead of me into the vestibule. He was used to low eaves. For me, despite my light clothes, it was an effort. A woman dropped to our feet to take off our shoes. In the shadow beyond the vestibule was another woman, much older—"Grandmother". The rest of the family was somewhere unseen. Grandmother was anxious about this visit. She was the most important person in the village. Hers was the most important family. She liked importance. She had waited many years for it. She had perhaps managed to live to an old age for it. She was anxious, yet she stayed decorously within the room, did not lean the least bit forward, and as we entered dropped back till she too was unseen.

I stepped into the room. The tall mayor knelt his way

into the room. The delegation followed, one man after another, one as formal as the other, one as silent as the other. Immediately the crowd in the street closed in on the house. Every cranny was occupied. The doorway, the vestibule, every opening, and from every projection of the neighboring houses yellow faces and squirrel-like eyes followed the scene. Each needed so small a space, and could hang in an awkward position so long, that it cramped me to watch. The school had been dismissed. The day had been declared a holiday. "Making a holiday when the eminent man comes is a way of inculcating morality," said the mayor. Then he explained that there had never before been a white man in Funakura, except a Catholic priest, and that the children later each would have one piece of bean cake.

Finally I was at the garden end of a large circle of Japanese gentlemen. For me there was a pillow. The porcelain figures bowed and bowed, and fanned themselves ceaselessly. The talk was in whispers, was passed along from man to man, reached the interpreter who was not very adequate, and the crumb that was left for me was some small formal phrase.

"We are honored by this coming of a friend of a friend of ours."

"We hope it has not been too hot."

"Too bad that the road is so dusty."

"It is a long way to travel."

"Not much here to give you."

"Not much here for you to see."

The talk went on that way, but it did after a while go easier, and it did somehow heat itself. The villagers were recovering their confidence. There was a swell, a swagger. One man insistently wanted to know what exactly were my reasons for coming so far to visit such a place—there must be very good reasons. One mentioned the Exclusion Act—growled. Another seconded the first. Several spoke at once. One told me that tomorrow he would show me the sword dance—in bad times the sword dance had often kept the spirit of the nation alive. One raised his voice and said that for scientists and artists there was no nation. One burst in, that even should there be war between my country and his I would be safe. One verified the last, assured me that undoubtedly I would be safe. One hastened to explain that the phrase "should there be war," meant not war exactly, but anything extreme.

There is an emphasis in Japanese talk—one hears it perhaps more plainly if one is anxious, as I was, and if one does not understand the words—and it wears somewhat as an insistent rhythm wears. The rhythms in Japanese music have that same general effect, as if more and something different were felt than could be said. That afternoon at Funakura it was the fire of the nationalism—and I think

they did not mind my sensing it, for this was Satsuma, and
Satsuma is franker in all ways than the rest of Japan.

I was as uneasy as I was that morning of my first arrival
in the country. Uneasy, and fascinated. I do not believe
that the Japanese have much human feeling for the foreigner. A curse on all their neighbors. I knew a New York
Japanese who would let people believe that he was quite
capable of doing them a dirty trick, that he had contempt
for their ideas, that he was really laughing in their faces.
And this was deliberate. I do not think he felt the contempt. It was simply his cool psychologic method. When
I hear atrocity accounts in the present war, where I believe
them, I always find it possible to imagine that the Japanese
might perform just that act. I never think the atrocity
lack of army discipline. I think it performed by command,
and publicized—to put crippling fear into our hearts. For
though we do not too much mind death for ourselves and
our families, we do shrink from terror and from mutila-
tion. I would think the Japanese would bayonet, choke,
break bones, slaughter, where they did these acts, by plan.
Not because they took joy in the acts, were cruel in that
sense, but the Japanese would certainly like to make Asia
unpleasant to us forever, and would not overlook the
psychologic ways of doing it, would be quite willing to
keep in our minds how diabolic a war they can and are
willing to wage.

Suddenly out of that circle of Japanese gentlemen one

called "*Banzai!*" Instantly each gentleman shifted from his haunches forward to his knees, the circle seeming to come down on me. Solemnly and marvelously someone pronounced my name. Solemnly and marvelously all pronounced it after him, on the last tone appeared to brace themselves, to set their faces, to suck a blast from somewhere deep below, then splattered forth: "*Banzai! Banzai! Banzai!*" It was the first free burst of flame, and it was damped as by a hand. It was like a drastic change of mood. One gentleman bowed low, addressed me formally. All the gentlemen bowed low and mumbled formally, and disappeared. I say disappeared, because the speed with which they went, the creeping silent speed, the collapsed bodies, the quick narrowing as they slid through the narrow doorway, made them for that moment ghosts. In the empty room a ring of empty teacups—the bulky bodies had moved as cats across a shelf of china.

In the garden there remained a boy, about ten years old. He moved in and out. He was noiseless. Once he looked at his face in the pool, or he saw a goldfish, dashed from the pool, serpentined between the lumps of lava that were the back wall of the garden, darted in and out among the dwarfed pines, and at last, with a spring that left his sandals behind him, mounted to where I stood. His dark eyes looked me over. He said something—and like a sprite was off again among the pines. Once again he looked into the pool. Such a boy-child brought up in such a room and such a garden, would have an eel-like body when he grew to be a soldier, could go on his hands and knees over a mountain or through a jungle into trailless territory impassable to an American or a European.

CHAPTER TEN
The 1927 Auxiliary Automobile Transport Facility Was 20,700

SUDDENLY THE FOLLOWING MORNING THAT BOY-CHILD broke out in a sweat of talk. The doctor interpreted. That boy knew more about automobiles than any boy I had ever heard anywhere—wore us out. For an hour—till we stopped him—he talked of models, makes, gasoline consumption, speed. He knew the world's record—it was made by an English car. He knew which was the next in order—that was a German car. But neither of these cars was yet on the regular market, he said, and of course neither of them had ever been seen in Japan. And of course, too, he had never seen any of the cars he was talking about. The first automobile manufactured in Japan was by the Tokyo Motor Car Works in 1909. But in 1927 almost all cars were still imported, which he emphasized was too bad, and must be changed, because Japan must never stop making progress. The number of cars imported in 1927 was 3,895.

The number of navy and army fliers to lose their lives in 1927 was 20. The auxiliary automobile transport facility in 1927 was 20,700 cars. This included private cars. In Tokyo alone there were 9,692. Finally I asked him whether he was going to be an automobile racer, an automobile merchant, an inventor, or a mechanic. He said: "No, I am going to be a botanist." Then he went right on talking of models, makes, gas consumption. Of fairy tales he knew nothing. Of poetry he knew nothing. I suppose you might find that kind of boy in any country in the world, yet queer to find him in Japan, in a village. "Ski" is the syllable with which he would dispose of model after model.

CHAPTER ELEVEN
An Unwelcome Guest

THERE WAS A SOUND OF *geta* ON THE GRAVEL. THIS was later in the morning. A kimonoed figure appeared in the vestibule. A kimonoed figure from the back of the house slid forward on its knees toward the vestibule, a servant. The two figures bowed. They spoke some low words. They bowed again. The one who stood passed his card, slid it over the *tatami* in the direction of the one who kneeled. The one who kneeled studied the card. Then he slid and walked, and slid and walked, until he was at the rear of the house, where two, then three studied the card, debated awhile in hissing voices. They could have been heard in the vestibule. Then he who had taken the card returned to the vestibule, and in a moment he who stood in the vestibule slid into the room. Then the host stamped in boldly from the back of the house. He dropped to his knees. The two men bowed. A question by the visitor. An answer by the host. A long interval. Another question by the visitor. A nod by the host. Another long interval. The visit was not going very well. A very long interval. The maid slid in with two cups of tea. The visitor bowed to the maid as he accepted the tea. Perhaps the host bowed, but no one could have been sure. The two drank the tea in silence. The visitor rose to a somewhat higher position on his knees, a gesture toward leaving. He mumbled. Surely the host must now protest at his visitor leaving so soon, but he did not. The guest backed out onto the veranda, and on out into the vestibule. A bow on the part of the guest. An exaggeratedly profound bow on the part of the host. The sound of *geta* on the gravel.

CHAPTER TWELVE
The Lord of Sendai

ONE AFTERNOON I WALKED OVER TO THE TOWN OF Sendai. Grandmother wanted me to go to see the shrine to Hachiman, the War God. She would herself have liked to go along, had gone often in the past, drew daily strength, she said, from the memory, but now she was ninety and it was not easy to go. The shrine was small and usual. On that particular afternoon a new cruiser, the *Sendai*, named after the town, had been ordered by the Admiralty into a nearby arm of the sea, and half of its crew had marched to the Hachiman to ask a blessing on the cruiser's history. The sailors were there while I was there.

The Lord of Sendai had been a million-bushel lord. That means he had a million bushels of rice a year—a million bushels left after his farmers each had taken his pittance.

And if one has a million bushels, surely one ought to be able to feed one's family out to the last adopted son of an adopted son. Wise to do it too. Wise to keep even one's

distant heirs in a good humor. Especially if one has a son,
a boy. Poison has been employed a number of times in such
cases. That, indeed, is the reason for the nurse. She takes
care. Nothing will happen to the boy while she is around.
Has she not a child of her own? Yes, poison has been tried
a number of times. In fact, no one eats the food brought
in from the kitchen. It is better to subsist on a bowl of
rice cooked right there in the room. The nurse herself
cooks the rice, and she keeps the boy always with her. The
two boys play together, hers and the Lord's, and when
anyone brings them sweetmeats, they refuse. It is sometimes not easy to refuse, and it is sometimes not easy to
get rid of the food that is brought in from the kitchen,
but one manages. Never has either boy eaten a mouthful
of that kitchen rice.

But this afternoon it is especially difficult. There is a tall
lady, and she is the aunt of the boy, and she has come in
her most beautiful kimono. She has a kind heart. She
brings the boy a cake. Of course, he refuses. No, but he is
too modest! He can have the cake. She brought it for him.
Certainly he can have it. He refuses. She laughs at him.
He refuses. It nettles her. What is this? He will not have
the cake brought him by his aunt? This is not right. This
is the nurse putting ideas into the boy's head. This is
rearing him wrong. His father shall know of this! This is
utter nonsense! He shall have the cake!

Suddenly the other boy, the son of the nurse, snatches

the cake out of the beautiful lady's hand—a thing unheard of!—eats the cake, and his small body just tips over, dead.

The nurse, his mother, utters not a word, not a cry. That was only what, in the last extremity, she had ordered the boy to do. That, in fact, had been the whole reason for having a boy. But when the beautiful lady—concubine of the Lord of Sendai, ambitious for her own son—when the beautiful evil lady is gone the nurse looks long, long, into the same dark corner of the room.

CHAPTER THIRTEEN
They Are Ready

I CAME BACK FROM SENDAI ABOUT ELEVEN O'CLOCK AT night. It was raining. Tomorrow was the *Bon*, the festival of the dead, and tonight there was the methodic preparation. All around the edges of the dim room stood the lanterns of the dead, some tall as standing Japanese, some broad as squatting Japanese, like mourners, fifty lanterns. It was a sister who had died within the year. Friends had given the lanterns. They might instead have given candles, or noodles, or rice. The rule is that each lantern be burned only once, but there are always the stingy, who cheat the dead, pass on one of their lanterns as a gift to another house.

I slept in the loft. The fourteen of the family all slept below. Outside it was raining. It had been raining three days. I lay down at midnight. At one o'clock the unfailing night-watch called something in the street. Grandmother was the only one in the house who really heard it. At two the night-watch called it again. At three the night-watch called it again. This time I heard it. "*O-miya!*" Water!

I leaned over and looked down into the room below. Everybody was awake. Everybody was at work. Each seemed to know exactly what he was expected to do. Silent work. Grandmother gave an occasional terse command. A few hours ago she had looked parched and done with life, now she seemed almost the youngest. The water was rising in the room. It was like an underground cave down there, the house boarded for the night, the eaves dipping all around, the still work going on in water, two lanterns of the dead sister at either end to furnish the light. The candles showed through the thin oiled paper, the shape of the flame, the white crest of the wax, the rest of the candle fading off in a fog. I began also to hear the water, flowing outside in the dark street, eddying in the garden, dropping monotonously from the sky.

They down there were systematically taking the house apart. It gave me a new idea of the Japanese house. We all know the style, but do not fully realize how practical a structure it is, how thrifty, how replaceable, how standardized. In Tokyo, or in the closely populated districts of Osaka, the houses may be shacks leaning on one another, two-storied, a thin frosting of stucco, and inside them industry and domesticity both going on at the same time. The more typical house, however, is one-storied, entirely wood, no cellar, no foundation, no solid wall. Even to this day a house may be stood up on hollow stones. By night

rough slides of boards are run in a groove all the way
around the edge of the house, barricading it from the
elements and robbers. The portable partitions between the
rooms consist of wood frames with opaque paper drawn
over them. The floor consists of *tatami*, six-by-three-foot
wood-framed straw mats, also portable, and resting on a
bamboo lattice. Rice paper serves for glass panes.

The work went on without waste. The strongest lifted
the heaviest loads. The children carried the china. Men,
women, children, two and two, boosted the *tatami* up into
the loft where I had been sleeping. Next the *shoji*, the
paper-windowed doors, were carried in stacks. Walls, partitions, floor, all were tucked up into the loft. There was
a space between the ceiling of the lower floor and the loft.
That is, there were two lofts, the first a consequence of
one high flood, the second the consequence of a still higher.
Water had been drawn from the well at the first warning
of the watch, and that now was carried up in wooden pails.
Rice had been rapidly boiled, and that was carried up.
Grandmother pointed to the charcoal and it was carried
up, and to the *urori*, the charcoal burner, and it was
carried up. She put four boxes of matches into the sleeve
of her kimono. The fifty lanterns all were carefully collapsed, and the children brought them to the loft. Grandmother watched the children, reflected how the lanterns
could not this night be offered to Buddha, saw how the
children worked with energy, said: "Their work also is an

offering to Buddha." Then she noticed how the bamboo lattices were beginning to be floated up by the rising water. She said: "As the water recedes, they will be floated exactly back into place." She herself dismantled the shrine and carried it up into the loft. One of the women rolled the *kakemono*, the painting, into a snug wooden box, later mounted the ladder with an armful of such boxes. All proceeded as if polished by experience, and yet it had been several years since the last flood. No one complained. No one seemed amazed. In any country, certainly, the first time you have water in your cellar you are distraught, and the fifth time philosophical, but what was queer about this methodic group effort was that there seemed no need for philosophy. Finally, the house, in skeleton, stood there in the dark and waters.

By noon the flood had risen to within eleven inches of the loft where I and the fourteen Japanese were huddled. Grandmother did most of the talking. It seemed with complete absence of emotion, just dropped her remarks around her. "Last year the water came within fifteen inches of the loft. . . . In 1921 it came within nine inches. . . . In 1904 it was five inches. . . . At three inches the house floats. . . ." My interest was emphatically in when the house would float and where it would float to, but that, judging by the faces, was my interest alone. A boy swam by, cautiously, because of the pell-mell of bamboo—once caught in that he would be as trapped as a rat. Another boy went by on

a raft. He called into each house. "Bigger than usual, is
the word from Miyanojo." Grandmother agreed. "The
bamboo never grows in the precincts of the shrine of
the Hachiman of Sendai, but this year it grew, and the
priest consulted the god. The god said: 'Big flood.' And
see!" A man swam by with a crying baby on his back.
Grandmother still was thinking and speaking, mostly to
herself. "Yes, very big flood—when it rises so around the
walls of the post office." The post office was diagonally
across. The postmaster had put on a straw hat like an
umbrella and serving for that, climbed out onto the roof
of the post office, let himself down into a boat, looked like
a figure in a play. "No earthquake now," said Grandmother, "but if there nevertheless should be—well, we
could pray." People were beginning to come out everywhere on the roof tops. That was because the sky had
brightened. They were saying somewhat fearfully—
and somewhat hopefully—that the flood might be so bad
that it would make a record. Blinking, clearing her ancient
eyes, remembering, thinking, speaking, Grandmother told
of the highest flood she could remember. They had already
dug a hole through the ceiling of the loft so as to be ready
to push the children out onto the roof, the *tatami* of the
loft were already afloat, and everybody was standing up.
Something that I suppose could have been accounted a
smile now came into her parchment face, and she turned
to me directly, emphasized with her hands, was interested

in what she was saying, and it annoyed her when the doctor intruded to interpret for her. She was saying that her husband, who was then still alive, the children's father, trembling, almost weeping, knee-deep in water, kept repeating: "Here am I to perish! Here am I to perish!" Again something that could have been accounted a smile, but what she said was that the village would now have a subject of talk for the rest of the year.

By four in the afternoon the flood stood still. It rained, but a very fine rain. "Rain of heaven," she said. Then she said that the valley was by now a great wash-basin and that a few more drops of water would not much change the level of the whole. The nickname of this small valley, she said, was "Anal-wash", because it was the low spot of all this region, and sure to have water. An old man, deaf, dazed, went by on a raft with his nephew who had saved him from drowning, was muttering: "Nothing did I do in preparation. And now, behold!" The sewage had been swept from the open sewers. That also floated by. The Japanese house is so very clean on the inside, so dirty on the outside, the "plumbing" so primitive, that when you live in such a village you simply cannot understand how this nation can have any mind for any mechanism not of wood, for any mechanism therefore of war. Which makes it only the more disconcerting that it should have.

A dead body from a new grave floated by. A man who was trying to save some logs was swimming after them and

yelling: "Rope, rope! Will no one give me rope!" Grandmother looked about her ruefully. "And this year the
flood came up slowly. Usually there is not even time to
boil the rice. It was too much time—so I forgot rope. I
always order them to bring rope into the loft. A bit of
rope is very useful." One of the men in the room just
rolled over where he was in the middle of the floor and fell
asleep. They had all been awake so many hours. His baby
daughter saw him. She looked at him seriously. She
moved over to lie beside him. I was thinking, how charm-
ing, when she pinched him in the side, brought him
with a start all the way out of his sleep. Then we all helped
to relay from house to house a sick man on a stretcher, to
get him to the doctor.

The rain stopped. The sun broke out. In the air birds
flew uneasily, so that their flight was more like the flight
of dragon flies. A pair of swallows was excited, went back
and forth over the same spot, must have had a nest under
the eaves. Then a whole flock of birds went to a tree trunk
where the rising water had driven insects from their holes,
a fact that the birds seemed all to discover at the same
moment, and even the two swallows took an interest.
Through the bird chatter broke the rough voices of men
directing one another at their work. At the very tip of one
roof stood a rooster, just could not understand it. The
small girl of the house, who had said nothing all day,
suddenly remembered the goldfish, and it was an un-

pleasant thought to her, they who were used to the quiet life of their pool, floated out into this muddy rushing ocean. Everybody's goldfish were lost in the flood. The whole village was distressed about it—very hard to pay for new ones. Grandmother said: "When the water recedes there will be many a carp trapped in the branches of the mulberry trees, and all one will have to do will be to go and pick them out." And down in the well, when the water was dipped out, as it would have to be to avoid typhoid, there would be more carp trapped.

Toward evening came a boat propelled by a boy. In the middle of the boat was a great heap of rice balls. Everybody was expecting that boat. It was the priest's. The temple stands at the highest point of the village where the flood reaches last. Whoever had no loft of his own had gone at once to the temple, and had carried along his belongings. So there was a great boiling of rice. And now the priest came up to the side of the loft, bowed, asked: "How many persons?" Grandmother bowed, counted: "Fifteen." The priest counted out the fifteen balls, passed them to her, she passed them to us, and soon all over the room we were munching cold rice.

By next morning the water had subsided, and, kimono wrapped tightly up around thigh and hip, the whole population went to work in the mud. It would be a month before the *tatami* could be put down, before the bamboo lattices would be dry enough, and if the *tatami* themselves

were wet, they would not be worth a *sen*. Everywhere there
was scrubbing, washing, sweeping, shoveling, the inside of
the houses, the outside of the houses. Every single person in
the village, young and old, was mobilized. In the tiny gar-
dens the women were smoothing the mud with their bare
feet. Everywhere the reflex manner of Japanese life went
on—everywhere the bodies bowed. They bowed from window to window. They bowed from rooftop to rooftop.
They bowed down to the passerby. For all the mud, for all
the grime, for all the dejection, for all the destruction, the
automatic manner went on. The night before I had looked
at the skeleton of this one house. Now there were half a
hundred such skeletons. For fifty thousand *yen,* the price
of a few rice fields, the village could permanently divert
the water, but even to talk of that was regarded as ridiculous self-indulgence. They were used to disaster and
seemed almost to choose not to avoid it.

CHAPTER FOURTEEN
Bamboo and the Bath

That night of the flood there was no bathing. Everybody in the loft was restless about this. I was always being invited to the bath. The guest bathed first, then the males in succession of age, then the women, last the servants, and the interest of this hierarchy gains when I add that, though one soaked and scrubbed in a pan, then rinsed with panfuls of water, the final rinsing was in a tub, and the tub was changed but once a day. Rigid method, rigid order, in the bath as in all else. The tub was small and keg-shaped, and heated below by a stone that was heated by a charcoal fire. The private bath of some houses was a wooden-walled pool that was large enough to swim in, but the routine remained the same.

In volcanic regions the water is brought to the bath in bamboo pipes that run down the hillside from hot and cold springs, an extraordinary casualness about the piping. Where length of pipe meets length of pipe—that is, where bamboo trunk meets bamboo trunk—there is a small wooden box to serve as a joint. This reduces the loss of water to the minimum, and, in most such regions, there is of course water to spare. If the water in your bath is too hot you push the hot-water pipe out the side of the bath-house, and bring in the cold-water pipe. As easy as that. The Japanese handle bamboo so much that they can make it do anything, and they handle it with that indifference. Bamboo for food, bamboo for house construction, bamboo flattened into sheets and made into boxes, bamboo for tobacco bags as soft as cloth, bamboo to lighten the zero fighting plane, bamboo for water supply—it is a simple economy. The hot spring means, besides economical cleanliness, economical free heat, a way of keeping the body warm in a variable climate. The house tub serves the same purpose, and it is perhaps its main purpose, defense against the cold that the Japanese does not bear well.

The ancient Japanese thought he washed himself clean of his bad doings. The cleanliness of the people is part of their sense of superiority over other Asiatics. It is part of their confidence that they will dominate other Asiatics. Like the Chinese, they think we smell, and it is true that the Japanese body is remarkably odorless—which does not mean the Japanese village, not the Japanese town, not the Japanese city, not the Japanese house, but only the Japanese body. It is curious how Japanese cleanliness may be undone when you surround Japanese with carpets, chairs, soap dishes, toilets, sinks, and Western enamel bath-tubs.

But in their own surroundings they can be very crowded
and still be very clean. Where we ate we had to sit so
close that we touched, the space left for eating was that
small. And the space for cooking was yet smaller. In fact,
the circumstances here made it necessary that the family
be even cleaner than most Japanese families, therefore it
was. Every person in the house changed his kimono invariably twice in the day, and always before the evening
meal. The bathing was literally clocked. And this discipline
fitted into all the other disciplines, and thus even the bath
becomes a part of the reason that the nation can be easily
regimented.

The day after the flood I bathed at the public bath. It
was a shack with a tall pipe in one corner, pale blue smoke
coming out—a characteristic detail of every Japanese city
or village. A servant brought me a straw basket, in it a
towel, a wash rag, a bran bag for scrubbing, a fresh kimono. I took off my clothes, then proceeded naked over
a runway across an inside garden. It was evening. There
was only a half-light. I was hurrying along the runway,
the basket shading the critical parts of me, when a
woman, entirely unshaded, came toward me. She was coming from the bath. I was going toward it. We crossed about
halfway along the runway and both of us bowed. Afterward, in the midst of my bathing, there arrived an oldish
woman, said she would help me scrub my back. I told her

I could not give her that trouble. It was no use. Her mind was made up.

The brown-yellow bodies would come out of the scalding bath a blustering, confident, glowing, puffing, red. That had visible psychologic effect on the personalities. On me the effect was something else. I saw mainly the smallness of the bodies. There are large-bodied Japanese, of course, six foot and even more, but most are small. The fisherman was magnificent but not tall. I had occasion over a long period to watch a small-bodied Japanese and a large-bodied American, the Japanese always detesting the American, who was superlatively large and utterly unaware of the Japanese. It was simply the psychology of a body mass that was actual, not overfed or overdeveloped, against a body slightness that was actual, entirely healthy and trim but slight. Both were real. And that makes a situation impossible for the slight. The one man's neck was like the other man's wrist. The experience with those two leads me to a comment that I realize may be entirely irrelevant or impractical. But, if I were a general on the Japanese front I would send wherever I could, large-bodied troops, though their movements were less agile. And I would send always ominous masses of troops, wherever the character of the battle made that practical, being at the same time scrupulously careful never to do so when this gave a feeling of baggy bulk. On the contrary, I would never send small-bodied troops if I could help it, even though they might be agile enough, and though my temptation might be to match agility with agility. Because our agility cannot ever equal their agility, whereas our mass, when it is mass, is apt not only to overpower but to freeze their agility. Against average-sized European troops the body difference would never be great enough to factor psychologically, but it might against a five-foot nation. On the contrary, if I wanted sympathetic reception for an envoy I would choose him small. Furthermore, I would never where it was not absolutely necessary employ a nibbling variety of attack against the Japanese opponent. He understands the nibbling—its use and its weakness and where it should be used. I would strike him with mass— and only when I had that mass. I suspect that this is basal in all military attack, but somehow more basal here. I believe the Japanese would show a disposition not to understand sudden mass, to be bewildered by it, to become panicky under the impact of it.

CHAPTER FIFTEEN
A Simple Suicide

THERE HAD BEEN A SUICIDE. THE JAPANESE CALL THIS kind a *shinju*. It was in no way extraordinary. It was the sort of suicide occurs in your own suburb. A girl and boy fell in love. The parents said no. In the Japanese village —not in the metropolis—that is usually final. So the two decided to make the journey to their ancestors. A river runs by the town, the same that caused the flood, but was well down into its banks again. The two forded the river. On the other side they looked about for a proper tree. He helped her up—hanged her on a branch. But when he saw her up there he did not think he wanted to follow her, so he came back across the river. Funakura hissed with gossip. Most everyone agreed that there was no "trickery"—the girl was not murdered. It was suicide. And it was natural suicide. But should he have let her go alone? Should he have entered such a pact and changed his mind? The girl, of course, had to die first—that was perfectly realized— but he had no right to lose his composure just because he saw her hanging. If he knew he was sensitive to a sight like that he should have tied his body to hers and tumbled the two of them over some high place. The possibility of his going back and completing the deed apparently did not occur to anyone. He was not arrested. There was no legal process then, and I think there was none later. It was simply that a number of very active questions had been raised. And new ones were constantly discovered, and the talk went on day and night, and day after day, and night after night, and the boy was right there in the midst of the talk. No one seemed to think that it would be an especially black mark on his life.

CHAPTER SIXTEEN
The Lantern-maker

Two small spurs ran off the single street. The lantern-maker's shop was at one intersection. There were, in fact, two lantern-makers in this village of six hundred, meaning one-third of one per cent of the population was engaged in making lanterns. Today Japan is a nation of one hundred million, as they claim, making cannon.

The starved-looking lantern-maker was a very dextrous creature. His shop being at a corner, you could look into it from two sides and watch him work. He squatted in the middle of his floor like a craftsman in a Hokusai print. He was not a great lantern-maker. The finer lanterns were bought in Kagoshima, or came from Osaka and Tokyo. Down here in Funakura the lanterns were sold for twenty *sen*, were of only a few forms, one color, one ideograph.

The man worked at a kind of potter's wheel. On the wheel he had mounted the form about which he was to shape the future lantern. It was at the moment a round lantern, and the form consisted of six collapsible leaves attached to a central axis. On the outer edge of these leaves, at intervals of an inch, were notches. On the floor to one side of the craftsman was a spool of bamboo thread —bamboo drawn to the thinness of thread by pulling thin sticks of it through smaller and smaller holes in a metal plate. He took hold of the end of this thread, started it at the upper notch on one of the blades, gave the form a spin, and perfectly guided the thread from one level of notches to the next, so that in less than a minute the lantern stood there in outline, just the ribs. Still holding his end of thread, he slapped a wooden hoop onto the top of the form, glued tight the thread, held this an instant, then nipped off the thread at the lower end of the lantern, inverted the form, slapped on the lower hoop, glued that, righted the form, returned it to the potter's wheel. So machine-fast was all this that the eye had trouble to follow. On the floor to the other side of the craftsman was a spool of cotton thread. Using now his left hand he took hold of the thread, began it at the top and laced it in and out the successive bamboo ribs, down to the bottom, fastened it, up to the top, fastened it, and so on. Fantastically neat. Dismally mechanical. There was now a ribbing of bamboo going one way, a ribbing of cotton thread going the other. Casually he picked up a sheet of rice-paper from a heap of such sheets, tossed it on the skeleton, ran his two hands around, and the paper lay there like a skin. Then a drop or two of paste. Then a moment for drying.

Then a dip of his brush into the inkpot—an ideograph, a big black Chinese character, leapt onto the skin. Then over the whole a drop or two of oil. The lantern was complete.

The Japanese has always seen his production world small—small objects. He strives of course to see it large. But the pattern in his brain is small. There is no question but that the Army and Navy and the industrialists charged with supplying these have in recent years strained to see in our dimensions. And it cannot but be said that they have done well, yet it keeps bearing the relation of a sandlot baseball game to that of a big league. To put it differently, just as Japanese life and story and history fill the Japanese mind with patterns for personal courage, for the application of tremendous effort for sustained periods and apparently beyond the limits of our endurance, so also that brain has in it ancient and modern patterns for carving *netsuke*, producing numberless bamboo canes labelled "Made in Japan", planting by hand, making tools by hand, keeping these tools in repair for a lifetime, fabricating frail paper lanterns, etc. I do not mean to say that that mind is incapable of a larger plan, but that a larger plan represents continuous strain, should fatigue the mind sooner, should make it break sooner. The reader will say that the pattern for Empire in that brain is decidedly large, maniacally large. True. For in that this brain has had endless training. From the very beginning his Emperor

has been to the Japanese the Emperor of the world. Therefore seeing Empire is easy and natural, as is also the ambition to move out and grasp Empire, but the means
whereby that may be accomplished in the modern world—
the mechanical method—has nothing but tiny models, the
tiniest, to go on. For tiny and delicate has been the characteristic of Japanese workmanship throughout its history.
I call careful attention, at the same time, to the ever-
present fact of the powerful Japanese calf muscle revealing itself suddenly through the kimono slit. That is, we
must not take any comfort too easily, not hold to any pet
theory too stubbornly.

I was walking in the street. "That lantern at the roof
edge," said the doctor who was walking next me, pointing to a yellow cylinder with one pitchy ideograph at the
middle of it, "how long do you think it has hung there?"

Seeing it was thickly oiled, I ventured it might be as
much as a year.

"A year! Seventy years. It was put there to mark the
day Sizuka was betrothed. That was in the tenth year of
Meiji."

Sizuka hobbled from the house in a stiff sky-blue kimono. I knew her. She was the one came regularly to visit
Grandmother—obeyed the rule that it was she who did
the visiting because it was she who was two years younger.
Grandmother always let her do the talking, then would
finish off the talk with a conclusive sentence of her own.

She completely dominated her friend. Grandmother was
ninety. The friend was eighty-eight. The friend seemed
to have such an unusually high forehead, but that was
only her severely-drawn hair, and her eyebrows that
were plucked. She had blackened teeth. Sizuka's family
had lived seven hundred years on that one small spot of
ground. (No one seemed exactly to know how old Funakura was, but everyone seemed to know that there had
been no increase in population in the last four hundred
years.) Sizuka had watched one generation troop off to
the Great War, an earlier one to the Russo-Japanese
War, a still earlier to the Sino-Japanese War, had lived
through the Rebellion, the Restoration, the Revolution,
had been in Funakura when Commodore Matthew Cal-
braith Perry put in at Tokyo Bay.

Sizuka, squatting back in her house, had overheard that
the foreigner had remarked that her lantern was very old.
She would make a gift of it to the foreigner! I was frightened at the idea, hurried to assure her that I could not
allow her to do anything so unusual. She smothered any
discussion, with a club knocked the picturesque object from
its fastenings, presented it to me with its past and its
cobwebs.

CHAPTER SEVENTEEN
1853

For MORE THAN TWO CENTURIES BEFORE 1853 JAPAN was sealed to the outer world. The reasons for the sealing are partly obscure, partly clear. Obscure where they lie in Japanese nature. Clear where they represent the practical plan of the early Shoguns to consolidate Japan within by not allowing her to be influenced from without. There were slighter reasons. An envoy was sent to Europe and brought back a not very pretty picture of European society. Will Adams, the shipwrecked Englishman who became the friend of the Shogun Iyeyasu, reported the Catholic church in an unfavorable light. Within the country there were continuous squabbles between the various missionaries of the Christian churches. The Christian missionaries furthermore were disposed to take more seriously their own superiors than the authorities of the country. And, finally, there was discovered a conspiracy among the Christians to overthrow the Shogun. This all occurred in the first half of the seventeenth century. Earlier there had

been a tendency of the Japanese to move abroad, to trade
with China, the South Seas, even with the West. An envoy
had been sent to the Vatican. A Japanese organized all
the Japanese in Siam to help the King of Siam to quell
a revolt, married a royal princess and became Prime
Minister of the Kingdom. Had this tendency succeeded
instead of that toward isolation, the history of the world
would obviously have been very different. Instead, however, the country was not only sealed but hermetically
sealed. One port, Nagasaki, remained open, under most
minute regulations. A few Dutch ships were allowed to
enter in the course of a year, eventually only one ship a
year. A small Dutch colony with its factory was allowed to
remain on the island of Deshima, which is six hundred feet
long and two hundred and forty feet wide, and it was
virtually under prison rule, no Japanese except guards or
traders with permits being allowed near, and now and then
a prostitute. Fierce laws proscribed in every kind of bloody
way even the slightest contact with the foreigner. Japanese
citizens were forbidden to leave the country. If any one
of them did, on his return he was executed. The building
of ships large enough to go abroad was forbidden. The
ships already built were destroyed.

And so for more than two hundred years the nation,
as is usually said, and as is by no means true, slept.

The outer world meanwhile was changing. Steam became the motive power of ships. Ships went farther and

more frequently. So there were shipwrecks. When these occurred in the waters around Japan the victims were not humanly received. If a ship had to put in at a Japanese port it was allowed nothing but water and provisions. The whaling expeditions of American seamen carried them in increasing numbers into the seas around Japan. Seventeen millions of American capital was invested for whaling in Japanese and Chinese waters. During the one month of April, 1848, nineteen foreign ships passed through Tsushima Straits, and Japanese coast guards spotted eighty-six foreign ships passing one Japanese port in the one year, 1850. Naturally there were "incidents."

There was also a great growth of curiosity about the island empire. The world was generally being subjected to human examination, exploitation, colonization, and the mere fact that there was such a walled people was irritating. This may even have been a principle prod to force open the ports.

Within Japan the isolation had bred a psychology. The Japanese were jealous of their isolation. They knew less and less of the outer world, so developed a contempt for it. They magnified their own superiority, much as an individual may when he isolates himself. That is, they were taking on both the strength and the weakness of isolation. Isolation had become an emotional matter. The Japanese soil was sacred and must not be defiled by foreign feet. Myth and truth about their origin and their history be-

came so mixed it all grew into a fabulously curious muddle
—still at present rather literally believed in, or pretended
to be believed in, by Japanese university professors.
Whether or not the outer world had a right to disturb
this seclusion can be argued. The Japanese say down to
this day, no. It has always been an angry point with some
of them. But that the isolation would have been broken
anyway is perfectly clear.

With the settlement of California and the movement of
Americans out into the Pacific, it was natural that American adventure should think of Japan. There were a number of attempts to open the ports. The American government supported an expedition that failed. Perry profited
by this. He got his idea along about 1850. And he was
the first man who had the patience, the resolution, the
persistence, the shrewdness and the talent for the task. He
also had some understanding of its magnitude. He never
thought that one ship with the bare courage to sail into
a Japanese port would have any hope of success. It must
be a visible fleet. He believed that a definite show of force
was necessary. He prepared accordingly. Andrew Jackson,
Zachary Taylor, James Fillmore, the successive presidents,
were all in favor of the idea. Daniel Webster selected the
convenient incident. "This incident may afford a favorable
opportunity for opening commercial relations with the empire of Japan, or, at least, of placing our intercourse with
that Island upon a more easy footing."

So Perry had the support of the nation. He also had difficulties. There were exasperating and complicated details, and expensive ones. For instance, the Dutch charts that were used in his expedition cost the American government thirty thousand dollars. Coaling vessels had to be arranged for the long journey. Perry did not want the coaling to be left to routine vessels. He wanted nothing to miscarry. It took many months of persuasion to bring together the four ships that were to form his first expedition. He thought there should have been more. He had been promised a squadron of twelve. But even the four did not get quite ready. For all his capacity the arrangements continued to lag. He grew restless at further delay, finally set out in advance and alone, in the *Mississippi*. He touched at Funchal, Madeira, St. Helena, Cape Town, Mauritius, Ceylon, Singapore, and Hong Kong. The three other ships later joined him, and when at last he entered Yedo Bay it was with two steamers and two sloops, the *Mississippi*, the *Susquehanna*, the *Plymouth*, and the *Saratoga*. Fuji came into sight on the afternoon of July 7th, and the ships dropped anchor off the headland of Uraga.

These were the first steamships ever to be seen in those waters. He placed them broadside to the land, so as to make them look as formidable as possible. He ordered port holes opened and the guns run out. He ordered no communication with or from the shore.

Perry's idea was to behave as "Japanese" as he could contrive. Therefore he carefully concealed himself within his cabin. He became a "sacred person." When a representative was sent from the shore he was not permitted to see the "sacred person." The language difficulty was great, but this added to the possibilities for stage play. At the same time Perry was scrupulously careful, and it was wise, not to let his sailors get into any kind of trouble with the populace in the small boats that were continually plying about the "four black ships." Even the Governor of Uraga was not permitted to see Perry—but he was permitted to get a glimpse of the gold box that had in it the letter from the President of the United States. Perry employed a quiet but unrelenting stubbornness. He said that the letter from the President was to be delivered to no one but the Mikado. It was suggested by the Japanese representative that Perry take his ships to Nagasaki. Perry said he would stay in Yedo Bay. He was asked to wait four days for an answer. He said he would wait three. He was asked not to allow his sailors to chart the waters of the bay. He said his sailors would chart the waters of the bay. When the Governor wanted to do business on the third day, a Sunday, Perry would not do business—the Sunday also became a piece of the stage play. The Japanese from the shore watched the Sunday service with their glasses.

That shore was a mystery to Perry and to his men and to the whole outside world. But the "four black ships" and the world beyond that they represented, were a mystery likewise to the Japanese. Indeed the shock of those "four black ships" was so great that it would have the power to keep shocking the Japanese through many generations. All who could crowd to the headland of Uraga were there. They watched every move of the foreigner. They saw with their actual eyes. But such was the intensity of the feeling that in far-away Satsuma they also saw. Perry brought with him the newly-invented telegraph, the Japanese had only fire signals, but the whole nation knew almost instantly everything that was happening.

When after many goings back and forth the negotiations had come far enough, the hour arrived for the Americans with their gold box to go ashore. Small boats of sailors went on ahead. A landing of straw mats had been arranged. The moment when the first white man, Captain Franklin Buchanan, stepped from the landing onto the sand, a visible and audible and ominous excitement ran through the watchers. Japanese soil, sacred Japanese soil, had been defiled, and that this feeling was no mere literary invention the ninety years since have amply shown. The revenge there sworn has been renewed again and again, sometimes lightly behind a smile, but often with much of the old feeling still somewhere close about. When Perry, who had remained incommunicado and invisible up to this moment, stepped from his flagship, the guns of the four ships sent out such a volley the Japanese found it comparable only to heavenly thunder. Perry had steamed his flagship to a point opposite the pavilion, placing that within range of his guns. The Japanese knew now what guns could be and what protection they could afford. They were not to forget.

Perry had a perfect sense of the drama. Every one of his men was visibly armed, also the musicians. To either side of him marched two black negroes, armed, to defend his person. The Japanese had never before seen such blackness. At length, the procession arrived at the pavilion that had been hurriedly built. Perry sat down like an Emperor. The Japanese acknowledged the letter of the President by a receipt. In this acknowledgment it was pointed out that the letter, which by Japanese law should have been received at Nagasaki, was received here at Uraga in opposition to Japanese law. There was a concluding sentence. "The letter being received, you will leave here." And so the landing party quite willingly did. Perry announced that he would return in the spring of the following year, and eight days after they entered Yedo Bay the "four black ships" sailed away.

In the succeeding months the island empire burned with discussion. The Shogun, who would have to face the foreign guns, knew that this was impossible, therefore was in favor of making a treaty with the foreigner. Instantly the southern clans were against making a treaty, as was the Emperor in Kyoto, as were all who stood on the side of the Emperor against the Shogun. In Funakura they argued one side and the other. "If the foreigner is let in, it will go with us as with our dogs, that once were pure breed and had ears that stood straight up, and now have ears that all hang down." "Anti-foreign" and "proforeign" were hurled back and forth and divided the country. But the most enlightened opinion was in favor of the treaty. Satsuma pretended, for local politics, not to be in favor, but was. Saigo from his youth had kept teaching that Japan's isolation was no longer tenable, that Japan must open its ports. He even made advances on his own. He sent a gift package to France. The package contained a medal beautifully struck off, a piece of Satsuma pottery, and a crude pot marked *Japanese sauce*. If the French happened to like the artistic taste of his people, they might like the gustatory, so he was sending them a sample of both.

But it is interesting to summarize what perhaps was the majority opinion of the enlightened of the country. It was this: to treat with the foreigner, learn his methods, and later, if it was so desired, use his methods to drive him out, or, if not so desired, use his methods to expand into his world. The Japanese have admitted that frankly right down into our own day.

Perry returned before he said he would, in January instead of April, and this time he proceeded up into Yedo Bay to where he could hear the bells of the temples of the future city of Tokyo. He had seven vessels instead of four. The Japanese fully intended to yield, could not do otherwise, but Perry did not know this, and the edginess of everyone at the second meeting is shown by a small occurrence. The negotiator for the Shogun, when he was about to put his elaborate eyeglasses on his nose, closed his fan as a first step, and did it with a crack, and instantly the American sailors had their hands on their guns. The negotiator smiled. Everybody smiled. The treaty of peace and amity was signed, guaranteeing the opening of the ports of Shimoda and Hakodate for anchorage to American ships, guaranteeing shelter to the shipwrecked, and coal, water, and supplies to passing vessels. This was the Western toe hold. There was still no provision for trade or consular officials, but that would follow. Japan had been opened. Later similar treaties were signed with England, Russia, and Holland. Satsuma soon after ordered and owned its first steamship.

So the Japanese opened the door of their country when Perry sternly knocked. It has been said that we got nothing and they got everything by the treaties, but the point is that the mass of the population did not want us at all. It was against the feelings cultivated during the long isolation. And the Japanese have never really fundamentally changed these feelings. They have never wanted the white. Today they may be hoping to close the door again—but of Asia. The counsellor who signed the post-Perry treaties was assassinated. It is said that when the present Commander-in-Chief of the combined fleets, Admiral Yamamoto, was asked why he chose the navy as a career, he answered: "I wished to return Commodore Perry's visit."

CHAPTER EIGHTEEN
Disciplined to Disaster

THE BUDDHIST TEMPLE GONG BOOMED ONCE. AFTER AN interval it boomed again. After another interval it boomed again. Kept that up. I had been sitting in the dim middle of the Funakura house, writing. I went out into the street to see. I realized afresh the character of that street—so narrow that you and your neighbor could have shaken hands without either of you stepping off your floor, and thatched roof touching thatched roof. People were standing, mostly silently, gazing off beyond the river, where, some miles away, smoke was rising. A fire. "Fire across the river—costly but pleasant to see," said one of the watchers, quoting. Presently here or there a man went into his house, came out with a wooden pail, walked off in the direction of the smoke. The temple gong boomed all day. Toward evening the refugees began coming, carrying rice bowls, *sake* cups, sticks of bamboo, boards of bamboo, much of this on their backs, and wooden clogs, straw mats, all that was portable in their houses. A man spoke to me, in that utterly expressionless way they often speak. "Children. Playing in the charcoal of the *urori*. Such discipline! Twenty houses burned to the earth. Lucky. If the wind had been the other way it would have been two hundred." His was one of the twenty. The smoke had died down.

Toward one-thirty the following morning I was roused by knocks. The event of the previous day had stimulated me to make an offer that was accepted in earnest. At two and again at three I must go the rounds of the village. I was the fire watch. He who woke me was the ropemaker, his the house next door, and with satisfaction he delivered into my hands two flat boards. He had just returned, in front of every house had struck the hour by clapping together the boards, so the good villager might know the time—might be reminded, as he turned in his sleep, of the folly of sleeping too soundly, the danger of fire never being far. What he said with each clap was: "Careful for fire." And he kept repeating this till someone inside answered—that is, someone inside had to wake. A round at two, another at three, then—with the whole village awake and amused—I handed on the boards, and so they went from house to house from hour to hour. They were the clapper of the village clock.

In the present war it has been proposed that we burn out the civilian areas of the productive regions of Japan, which means especially Osaka, Kobe, Kyoto, and Nagoya. This may or may not be a practical war measure, and one would need in any case seriously to consider its effect on permanent peace. Osaka has a war population of approximately three and a half million, Kobe and Kyoto approximately a million and a half each. There are few places in the world where the houses are more closely huddled than in parts of Osaka. The way the bent figures of workers are everywhere tucked in makes one think of life in a pigeon coop. It is suggested that incendiary bombs dropped indiscriminately on the civilian population from altitudes beyond anti-aircraft range would start enough fires to put to an impossible test the fire system of that inflammable city. It would burn like Coney Island, cut across the narrow canals, leave completely paralyzing destruction. There is here no question of burning out steel works or factories, which must be dug out with bombs, but just a question of burning the houses of workers and killing the families of workers, and perhaps driving whole cities into mad, stampeding, Judgment-day panic, as Tokyo is reported to have been driven by the Great Earthquake, thereby incapacitating the Japanese industries. Anyone who has seen the denser slum areas of Osaka, and has felt the general claustrophobic character of this so-called Chicago of Japan, must at once have thought of fire. Our fire departments would condemn most of the houses in that city.

It ought to be pointed out that the famous fires of Osaka are back thirty years, and that Japanese acumen

may now know somewhat better how to control fire.
(There was once a fire in old Yedo where more than a
hundred and eight thousand persons were burned to death,
all the bodies buried in one pit, where now stands the
Temple of the Nameless Dead, supported by the proceeds
from exhibitions of *sumo*, Japanese wrestling.) The Japanese must also be credited with foreseeing, after twelve
years of war in China and three years of war in Europe,
the effectiveness of incendiaries. It is impossible to think
that they have not anticipated the consequence to their
industries of wholesale decimation of their workers. It is
definitely known that they have trained every strong-
bodied civilian as an incidental fire fighter, and—this is
conspicuously Japanese thinking—"have even restricted
constructing of air raid shelters for civilians on the theory
that if civilians had no place to flee in an air raid they
would fight the fires." So some degree of protection not
apparent in a description of the huddled city must have
been achieved. But let us assume that the civilian areas of
these large productive centers could be burned out and the
workers killed or rendered helpless in such numbers as to
upset the morale in a way to bring the end of the war
nearer by months or even a year. That is, let us assume
the method practical as a war measure. Should we use it?

I think not. I think we are waging a war to achieve a
peaceful approach to the problems of the world—the per-
petual problems, the changing problems, the problems of

the future that cannot be anticipated, that must arise forever if man is to grow, that inevitably will create mental conflict that we hope not to have soon again boil over into physical conflict—and we ought not by the methods of the war to handicap for long years to come belief in the possibility of true peace.

Nearly eighty years after Sherman's march to the sea, the South is still resentful. That the march to the sea did have something to do with winning the Civil War for the North, brought the end nearer by months, cannot be doubted, but it delayed by decades the spiritual approach of North and South, which is not perfectly accomplished even now. No Southerner actually forgives the North if his grandmother remembers what her father said, or if he has read his grade-school history book. This is realized by all Americans. None of us now thinks that Sherman's was a wise method of war. And, realize, the South is just across the river. Movement in and out of the South began immediately with the peace. North and South spoke the same language, had the same previous history, the same traditions. If it was difficult for the North to win the sympathy of the South in the course of eighty years, what hope would America have of ever wiping away the memory of a quick campaign that burned out, not the rich estates and the rice fields of Japan, but the dwellings of the people with the people in them. Japan is six thousand miles away, speaks a different language, is a country that ninety

years after Perry we have penetrated comparatively tri-
flingly, and may possibly penetrate even less in the time
to come. If we hope to win the Japanese to a peaceful
way of living in the world—and so give a peaceful life to
our descendants—we had better not put a Sherman's
march bloodily into the children's primers. It will be said
that the Japanese wage just this kind of war upon the
Chinese. There is no doubt of it. Yet the question remains, will tit-for-tat warfare give us the only end we
are seeking in the war, peace. We are not in this war to
avenge Japanese military behavior in China, nor even to
repay them their attack on Pearl Harbor. We are in this
war to win, and then to force and lead the Japanese into
a relation to the world that may make it possible to live
with them. If there is no other way of winning than to
practice a Sherman's march to the sea, we might have to
adopt so fundamentally unsound a method, but we must
be pretty desperate before we try it. We must remember,
whether we like to or not, the difficult psychologic problem we are bound to have with an Asiatic nation that is
strong, and would be strong again a generation after defeat. All of which it behooves us to have in mind when
we contemplate, as has been suggested, a late August
afternoon, the weather dry, a light ceiling of mist hiding
the bombers, that with fifteen minutes of work, practically costless to us, will burn away the civilians of three
or four cities and with them, perhaps, the next one hundred years.

CHAPTER NINETEEN
Diogenes on a Straw Mat

GRANDMOTHER SPOKE EVERY NOW AND THEN OF HER husband. She left in me the memory of a Japanese village king that has its interest.

All his life he had said he would die when he was sixty-five, and so he did. To last as long as he said he would he had to outlive three apoplectic strokes, the first of these ten years before his death.

Early in life he had begun to drink, started every day at five in the afternoon, and continued until eleven at night, when he went to bed. He sipped very slowly, from a tiny *sake* cup, and the *sake* was very mild, so he was never intoxicated. In his last years he neither drank nor smoked, only sometimes asked that he be allowed to smell the bottle. Never in his life did he do any real work. All day long he sat on the same two *tatami*. They were his two *tatami*. He could not be moved. He never changed his kimono of his own accord. His wife would periodically tear one stinking garment off him and bodily replace it with another.

In the hills around Kagoshima someone found two sticks of wood. They were very old wood. When the grain marks were put together, it was seen that the sticks came from the same piece. What were they? No one knew. Everybody was consulted. Might they not be a relic of some importance? The Kagoshima gentlemen asked the opinion of all the antiquarians and sages and generals in that city. No one knew. Finally it was suggested that the gentleman go down to that small village, Funakura, on the other side of Sendai—and of course he down there did know. In ancient times such sticks were carried along into battle. If a samurai killed a great person, he plunged one of the sticks into one of the great person's ears. After the battle he laid claim to the honor of the job, and, if there was anyone who doubted, he plunged the other stick into the other ear and lifted up the body by the head. And if anyone still doubted, he let the grains of wood on the two sticks be compared. For the same purpose he might carry in a compartment of his sword two pieces of metal with a design one-half on each.

From all the *ken* people would come to ask questions of the man of the two *tatami*. Usually he answered them with an epigram. That is, he was not only village king but village sage, though not one thing would he have to do with the affairs of the village, except in the above-mentioned oracular capacity. "Shall we have a picnic tomorrow?" He answered yes or no. He knew which rains would bring flood, which rains would not. A weather question is all that would get him off the two *tatami*. He would take his walking stick, walk out into the garden, look at the western sky. There were five thousand acres of lowland on the other side of Funakura. When they filled that in, he always said, Funakura would begin to have floods. It did. He told that during the filling one girl was sacrificed—to complete the dam. Once there was a flood, and everybody wanted to begin taking the house apart because the water was rising so rapidly. He said, no. Everybody got more and more frightened. No. His wife got frightened. No. Apparently he had his eye on a small birdbath, knew how high the water had to rise in that before there was danger of water in the house. Another time there was a flood. A *tatami* got soaked. He insisted he would dry it. He burned one hundred cubes of charcoal, worked all day, squatting, and in the evening threw away the wet straw. In his house he was generally severe, though he said little. Out of his house he seemed timid. He was very poor. There were considerable moneys owing him from old loans in palmier days, but he made only the most formal attempt to collect them. Once in a year he sent out the bills, sent them with the perfunctoriness that his neighbors sent New Years greetings. He would indulge in prolonged academic debate as to when they should be sent. One would not, for instance, send them so that they arrived in the morning, because who wants a bill to begin the day with. And one would not have them arrive in the evening, because a man is then composing his mind to meditation or sleep. Meanwhile his wife was year after year making shift to keep rice and fish in the house, but he did not take that too seriously, thought it better for her to be doing it than for him. She earned the money by turning her house into a lodging for the night. In the course of his life he wrote about ten thousand poems. He began when he was young. He wrote the last just before he died. What they were worth no one really knew. All were sooner or later destroyed, usually by himself. But for some time after he composed them no person might touch them no matter where he left them—you have to know the Japanese house to realize how terrible this seems to a Japanese. He spread them anywhere, on the *tatami*, hung them on the *shoji*, dreamed in front of them, dreamed before he wrote them, while he wrote them, after he wrote them. In fact, dreamed. A storage house back in the garden had a large compartment full of his poetry, but no one ever looked there. Once long ago he had been the postmaster. But he wanted to write poetry, so his son delivered the letters. Finally the son became the postmaster. He trained that son to a knowledge of Japanese prints and Japanese paintings. He himself knew all the paintings of any distinction in the Oriental world—in copies. He encouraged his son, despite poverty, to buy Japanese prints, and constantly to improve his collection of copies. So good was his eye that a single false line would expose the imitator. This species of detective work was especially interesting to him, as to many Japanese. There is a wide knowledge of painting in the islands, and the knowledge of this Funakura stay-at-home, poring over his copies, illustrates it. His own writing was very much in demand for inscriptions on tombstones, both because of its quality, and because of his eminence. It was often the last request of the dying. His wife thought his memory almost eerie. He would ask for a book that he had not seen in years by saying that it was in the loft, give the shelf, give the number of volumes from the left or the right end. He expected the same memory in his children. Needless to say, he did not realize his expectation. But he did not let that upset him either. He knew too well the sorrows of fathers in the abstract to let them get to be an actual sorrow for him. If anyone asked him where a thing was, he invariably answered: "Where it belongs." His wife called him Mr. Proper Place. Something had to be found that was packed away in a chest. He would say: "The third chest." But there were fifteen chests. Which third? He would answer not another word. One of the children would have to search, all the while knowing that to handle something that belonged to the dead—and there was always something belonged to the dead—was a heavy evil omen. All day he read, sometimes all night, and remembered everything. Someone mentioned the great Daibutsu at Kama-kura, and he immediately told the history, like a guide, gave all the dimensions, said that the circumference around the thumb of the Daibutsu was exactly three feet. Naturally he was opposed to all education. Was he not the canniest in the *ken*, and had he had an education?

The present postmaster of Funakura told me confidentially he never knew a man who knew so much. True, his knowledge had not taken him far in the world. In fact, he never left the village. In fact, he never left his house. In fact, he never left his two *tatami*. Yes, he did once. He went to Kagoshima. It was when the husband of his daughter was dying. When the husband died he came right back. The postmaster compared him with the Zen priest on the rock island in Matsushima, who had not crossed the bridge to the mainland once in twelve years. The postmaster had never known a cleverer man. The clever man had himself discussed the point. Why should he travel? Did he not know that the world was everywhere the same? What he suspected was that if he were to leave Funakura and go to Tokyo, instead of being the sage of Funakura, he would be the sage of the Empire, and was it worth all the trouble?

He did not like the smell of babies, and that fact sometimes drove him from his *tatami*. He took no stock in religion. His wife, on the contrary, was recognized the most religious woman in the *ken*. Never once did he raise his voice in protest—her folly was at least her own affair. He would say she was an extraordinary woman. He would say she had shown great courage in the Rebellion, hid one of the rebels right there in the house, and then he would smile.

CHAPTER TWENTY
The Bombing of Kagoshima

PERRY HAD OPENED TWO PORTS. TOWNSEND HARRIS, THE first American consul, opened four more, and these the largest. Yokohama, Kobe, Nagasaki, and Niigata. Single Japanese were from the start trying to slip out of the country—these were the young and adventurous. One midnight two men appeared alongside one of Perry's ships, begged to be secreted, wanted to go to the West and bring home knowledge that their country could use, had the writing materials on their bodies to take down the notes. Perry felt sympathy for them, but made the two return to shore. One of the two for reasons of his patriotism was later beheaded. At the same time foreigners were beginning to come in—warily. The hatred of them was intense. They had forced their way into the country, and, with rare exceptions, the feeling continued to be that their intrusion would later be avenged.

There were many episodes. Of the following footnote to history I knew nothing when I went to Kagoshima,

though to Kagoshima it rated more important than the
Battle of Waterloo. I remember the tall citizen of Funakura who recounted what he believed were the facts, especially the dead way his long arms hung, and the way his
face did not move, and how nevertheless it transmitted to
me a sense of remembered violence and glee. A farmer.
Poor.

It was in 1862. The Lord of Satsuma was making his
annual pilgrimage from Kagoshima to Yedo. A parade of
swashbucklers, their native impertinence stepped up by
recent events. What they were saying to one another was
that there were too many foreigners on the road to Yedo
—the foreigners were beginning to think they could do
as they pleased! A stop must be put to it. The next foreigner who broke through the procession would be cut
down. That was the law. And who was to do the cutting
was to be left to fate—namely, the guard of the palanquin
where the breach occurred. That was agreed. The procession reached the hamlet of Namamugi. There were two
Englishmen and an Englishwoman watching. Richardson
was the name of one of the men. He had been in China.
You keep Chinamen in order by showing them who you
are. Why not Japanese? Narabara was the name of the
guard where the break-through occurred. He cut down
Richardson without a quiver.

My tall historian stopped to assure me that perhaps
Richardson did not know the law, which excused him. But

he was insolent, which made him worthy to be cut down.

There was trouble now. The deed occurred September 14, 1862. England threatened the Shogun, demanded indemnity, wanted Narabara handed over. The Shogun said the affair had nothing to do with him, nevertheless paid the indemnity, the coward! But England was not satisfied. Where was the murderer? The Shogun pleaded that he did not know. He referred England to Kagoshima. England must talk to Prince Shimazu, and to the Lords of Satsuma. The Lords listened but said they could do nothing. They said they owed no indemnity. They said that it was the law of the land that whoever crossed a Lord's procession was subject to instant death. That was the law. Did the foreigner insist that he could interfere with the law inside Japan? Would the foreigner suffer such interference in his own land? Behind their masks they smiled. But England was not satisfied. England continued to insist. There was delay after delay in the negotiations. Finally it got to be August, 1863. Part of the English fleet proceeded around the tip of the southern island, slipped into Kagoshima Bay. Ah, great England was at war with Kagoshima!

The tall historian was filled with excitement.

Kagoshima was filled with excitement—and perhaps a trifle nervous. Negotiations began once more. Among the negotiators, right there on the English ship, who do you think? Narabara. England wanted Narabara's head, and they had it, and they did not know they had it! Kagoshima negotiated. Kagoshima wanted time. (And, as the historian did not mention, the English commander was anxious not to fire the town if he could help it.) Activity on the shore was feverish. Kagoshima had a few cannon that she had cast herself. These were brought up. Soldiers were moved. The negotiations went on. Numberless small craft were always around the English warships. The English were hungry. The natives came aboard to sell them food. The English spread nails on the deck—a miserable trick!—so that the natives in their bare feet would be unable to attack. The feet of the foreigners had no toes, the natives reported—thought the shoes were feet. (Such a Gulliver's Travels idea of the Westerner was possible less than eighty years ago.) The natives had brought melons. The English were hard to please, wanted to drive a bargain. Impatiently the merchants slashed open several of the melons—with swords! Each evening it would grow warm. The natives would go swimming in the sea—not naked, the foreigners' sensibilities must not be shocked. Every man wore his loin cloth, but suspended from the cloths were the bared swords. Swam with their swords!

The negotiations went on. Then, one day, at the stroke of noon, without warning, in the middle of the negotiations, the forts opened fire. (The tall historian was so stirred by now that it would have been easier than ever for him to confuse fact and fiction.) Fearful consternation among the ships. And more fearful yet when from five points around the bay the cannon roared all at once. Those miserable natives had learned well from Commodore Perry! They were also able—half way around the earth from civilized England!—to fire big guns. (The surgeon that first night in Kagoshima, told me, even he with some disturbance of poise, how one gun was mounted on the sharp point of a saddle-back hill, and how each time it fired it rolled down, sank out of sight like a modern gun, actually rolled only on its own momentum and had to be pushed up again by human hands—but it mystified the enemy!) And what finally happened? Why, the English ships lifted anchor and fled! All but one. That one did not wait to lift anchor, simply cut the chain—a disgrace. The weather, too, had come in and helped with a gale. It was glorious. As for those guns all along the shore that the English saw with their glasses, they were not guns but gun-mouths made of Satsuma pottery! And all those men behind the guns? Straw! But a real gun or two there were still out at the tip of the narrows, and these as the English fleet passed through delivered a salvo of farewell.

That is the way the historian told it to me. And it is true that many English officers and men were killed, and that the ships never silenced the guns, and that Satsuma never surrendered Narabara. He later became governor of the Ryu Kyu Islands.

Manning one of the guns was a Satsuman who would

be famous in later Japanese history, Togo. He was there with his three brothers, and he was stripped to the skin, sweat pouring from him. He was sixteen. During the fighting a shell broke near him and in the flash of it he saw his mother. She was bringing her sons hot tea. And Saigo was there—recalled from exile in Oshima for the occasion. And every house in Funakura was represented. And every house in Sendai. Grandmother remembered it all as if yesterday. In the days after the battle she had a positive run of lodgers.

As for the anchor—the tall historian now spread both his long arms in a gesture of generosity—Kagoshima gave it back to the English, sent it to them, delivered it to them, and the next year Great England, very thankful, presented the Lord of Satsuma with a gift. A spinning wheel. That spinning wheel is in the museum by the two graveyards. Whoever wishes to see it may do so right down to this day. Satsuma studied that spinning wheel, imitated it exactly, made many copies. And sixty years later, "just about to the hour," Japan's textile industry exceeded Great Britain's.

CHAPTER TWENTY-ONE
They Ran in Formation

EARLY ONE AFTERNOON WE STARTED BY TRAIN FROM Kagoshima toward the base of Kirishima mountain. It rained. It rained increasingly. A village emerged from the rain, disappeared. A house emerged. Disappeared. Two bridgeheads loomed, grew clearer, and overhead rolled a train, no glass in its windows, the coaches jammed with sailors. Many along the road, especially the men, just let the rain pour down on them. Others carried big oil-paper umbrellas. Some were on bicycles. Much of all mechanical locomotion was on bicycle. The whole picture was disheveled, and yet the life in it somehow worked—hard for an American to believe or quite understand. At Kachiki an old man hobbled into the coach, mounted onto the seat beside me, fit his naked haunches between his naked heels, then, to cover his shyness, planted his hands squarely on his hips, boldly examined me, addressed me, presently revealed himself nervously eager that I should miss nothing, pulled me from one window to another, pointed where the labor in the fields and the movement along the roads went on despite the downpour. "The country is small," he explained, "not like your own. Every foot must be employed and the toil must be relentless." All over Japan, scientist to peasant, they liked to tell you this, were always at work at the impossible justification. Once out the window there was a woman, ancient, bent, trudging up a headlong path, a keg strapped to her back. Once there were two—the train had idled to a stop—walked slowly in a circle, shoved heavily on the arms of a windlass, drew five tons of lava over the resisting earth. *Yottoko-maitae*. One of the two exhorted the other. *Zutto-maita*. The other answered the one. Then back and forth and back and forth, a kind of litany. *Yottoko-maitae*. *Zutto-maita*. Remarkable words to the eye, and even more remarkable to the ear, though in translation nothing but an emphatic bidding, *Shove hard*, followed by an emphatic rejoinder, *I have shoved hard*. *Shove hard*. *I have shoved hard*. Inch upon inch the red mass yielded.

I had been offered a summer house high up on Kirishima mountain. The house belonged to the old Kagoshima doctor, father of that skinny boy who had followed me around with the umbrella. The skinny boy was conducting me—was having another chance to speak German.

We arrived at the base of the mountain. From the train to the automobile we picked our way through a corner of a town, the streets nearly impassable mud. Yet the women with white one-toed socks, *tabi*, pumped along on their clogs and never for some reason caught a splash.

The driver of the automobile was anti-foreign, frankly. He did not even like to be driving an American. But it was his job, he said, and once having stated how he stood seemed to feel better about the whole business. The son of the doctor told me everything the driver thought, also frankly. Once the son of the doctor remarked that Japanese Kultur was one-third Chinese, one-third European, one-third mud. He was young, a cynic. But the mud continued dreary truth. A lame man pushed through it. A dog. A child. We meanwhile drove wildly, I felt, in and out narrow streets, spattered anyone, everyone, people all backed against the houses,—the automobile climbed up and down over anything, a ten-year-old Dodge, and broke no axle though I did not see why—and came out on a mountain road. The son of the doctor remarked that the road would be possible for the automobile only part of the way. The rain by now more filled the air than fell. It was fog and rain. Then later there was only fog. The whole world settled indefinitely into this whey-colored medium. The boy regretted it in ceaseless German. He wanted fervently I should see the views. He explained that the word Kirishima meant "island in fog." He had been coming to these Kirishima hills all his life. If it were not for the fog we could see the ocean, wonderful vistas. Once the fog did break, and far out I saw a line of fishing

boats. But immediately the fog crept in again, thin fingers
in advance, and we were engulfed. Once an imbecile was
sitting by the side of the road on a stump of tree, his
legs dangling over a well of water, his eyes empty, his
face vacant.

The son of the doctor explained to me that fogs were
not common here in the southern island. And not common on the big island, Honshu. But in the north and on
the Pacific side, especially in Hokkaido and in the Kuriles
right on up to Kamchatka and to Bering Strait, there
was much fog and very bad weather, storms and cold. Ah,
but from the army's point of view, many kinds of climate
to draw on for its man power! In Hokkaido, for instance,
there were snows fifteen to twenty feet—good preparation
for fighting at fifty below zero in Siberia. How lucky!
Was that not lucky—that in the islands in the south, out
in the sea beyond Satsuma, there should be a gradual
preparation for jungle temperatures?

He worked every minute at his German. I wished he
would not try so hard. I remarked on how he tried. He
took it for a commendation. He told me that he also
played the violin. And he had made his violin—got the
directions out of a book. Next he had taught himself to
play, from gramophone records. He played something of
every great composer. He now whistled the themes to
prove it to me, and I recognized a fairly good ear, and
felt overwhelmingly the effort. He told me that he had

been rejected for the army—they wanted strong bodies and did not care about the minds. He played especially Kreisler—because Kreisler had made so many records. He broke off to remark that we were just opposite a fine waterfalls—too bad we could not hear it and we could not see it.

The Dodge could go no farther. Two rikisha runners were waiting. The rikishas had their covers up. The anti-foreign driver was glad to be rid of me, and said it. I asked the boy to ask the driver why he felt as he did, and the driver explained that it had nothing to do with affairs in the world right now, but that he was convinced that it would have been better to be a Satsuman in the old days, when the ports were still closed, when Japan was a less effeminate country. But he was glad that there was no Shogun and that the Tenno had all the power. (The Tenno is the Emperor.) And when he had said that he walked away without adieu and without apology.

We continued the ascent. The young man read the signs on the trees, called over to me. The signs were telling how far we had come. Twelve hundred feet. Thirteen hundred feet. Fifteen hundred feet. It was never believable that a human machine could keep up that pace, dragging a car and a human body and some baggage, the path uneven and twisting in and out and around the vegetation. I kept staring at the bulging calves of the short legs of the runner, the skin shiny with sweat and rain. The runners all die early, they say, of heart ailments or of tuberculosis.

We continued the ascent. Off a short distance between the trees, through the pathless forest, over the wet slippery ground, appeared a company of boys, or young men, running, keeping the space between them equal. They were running in formation up the mountain. I did not know immediately what it meant—young men running in the rain and fog up a mountain with their heavy belongings strapped to their backs. The top of the mountain was their destination. They were in training for the army.

There was a brief break in the weather. It inspired my friend to ask the runners to take us to the top before we went to the house. The runners did not care to but they took us. They cared to less when the rain came down again. Then the rain stopped again and the fog thickened. Furthermore it was growing dark. The pines loomed a moment, faded out. My friend called over, read aloud a sign of the Forestry Department: "Spare the tree, even the smallest, for it may one day become the mast of a ship." Suddenly the earth was bare. No vegetation. The runners could not take us over that, and we had to walk, a cruel climb that appeared to lead nowhere, till, almost by a step, below us, wondrous desolate, silent, lay an absolutely round crater lake, truly round as a coin.

Onami was a princess, daughter of the lord of all the valleys and the seas beyond here. Once a year the men, her brothers, braved the wildernesses and the steepnesses, made the ascent from their palaces down at the sea near Kagoshima, up to this quiet pool, not far from where the first god—great grandfather of the first Emperor, father of the war god over there at Sendai—set his foot on fog or earth or water, whatever element it was, and spoke the words, and unrolled the mist, and so stretched out before him all the land of Japan. Once a year her brothers went, and once a year returned and related all that had transpired, and filled the mind of the maiden Onami with a lingering longing. But year after year they would not grant her wish, denied her the right to brave the wildernesses and the steepnesses. She brooded and she waned. They saw it. It was her fifteenth year. They took her with them, and she braved the wildernesses and the steepnesses, and stood at last at the brink of the pool. There was not a murmur there. It was bleak and barren and there were no birds, and something about the maiden as she stood made the rough men muse. Suddenly, suddenly, she rushed forward and flung herself into the still water and like a stone disappeared. Only a silent and mystic oscillation of the surface. Madly the men rushed about, hither and thither dove into the water, called their sister by name, but to no avail. They could not bring themselves to believe this was the end, and stood on the shore and cursed and called, and were silenced only when out of the water, where Onami went down, rose a dragon, fierce and sedate, who slowly looked about him and forthwith sank again.

We stood gazing into the pool. The young men whom we had seen running up the mountain, stood there also. One of them said: There was something in that pool that drew you toward it. And he looked away. It was so still, so evenly round, so red, and while we gazed half of it disappeared in a wall of fog, as if a curtain had been dropped, and a fresh burst of rain drove us back to the rikishas.

The descent was difficult. Furthermore it grew dark. By the time we reached the house it was black night. Two strange mountain folk came out with yellow lanterns. Both were old. The woman had gaping teeth, and two scrawny legs uncovered far above the knees. The man must have had his head squeezed in the womb, so flattened side to side as to suggest a flattened stove pipe, with the result that his eyes, which were really quite normally placed, seemed to lie in the middle of his head. They were in-turned, and he had some difficulty about opening them. They would get caught and start and get caught again, like poor curtains, a difficulty that had given him the habit of looking from under at you. There was much eye disease all over the country. The woman had it too. But formerly there was more. Each time I turned to look at the man I found those two bloodshot inrolled binoculars examining some aspect of my person.

CHAPTER TWENTY-TWO
The Family

THE NEXT FOURTEEN DAYS I PASSED IN THAT HOUSE on that mountain. It gave me yet another idea of the Japanese family unit. It is a close-knit formidable structure.

There were eight children in the house, all girls. Seven were the children of one daughter-in-law, one the child of the other daughter-in-law. Every morning and every evening the children played games. Usually it was pat-a-cake first. Two would begin it. In fifteen seconds there were twos all over the room. The children were animal-quick with their hands. You watched them with your eyes and with your ears, as you watch gypsy children use castanets. Constantly changing wild rhythms. A surprising thing would happen. The two would be playing on their knees. One would roll over backward, her partner would roll over backward, and instantly the same animal-quick pat-a-cake with their bare dark feet.

Next they would play a game that children in the West play also, except that the Japanese girl would drop a fan

instead of a handkerchief as she ran around the ring. Only
the smallest did not play. At least she never began any
game when the others began it. Some shyness intervened.
Her father would squat in a corner and look on, and she
might come and lean against his knee. But at length she
would desert him. She would let herself be drawn step by
step toward the whirl of the ring, suddenly would break
through the ring, drive out whoever was kneeling in the
middle. There was each time such a feminine directness
about the way she did it that the others laughed. She
never knew why they laughed, but they laughed, so she
laughed too. She would squat there in the ring awhile.
Soon, however, she would weary of that, would fling
herself in the path of her who was fleeing with the fan,
would demand the fan, would open it, close it, open it, close
it, toss it with abandon into the air. Her own movements
would intoxicate her. She would dash through the ring.
She would dash around the ring. She would snatch the fan
a second time, hide it in her kimono, run a quick short
run, and bow like a prima donna.

For the other girls this had not the charm that it had
for me. She had spoiled their game. She spoiled it every
morning and she spoiled it every evening, and one of them
pushed her off to one side, and immediately a small pene-
trating wail went into the air. Quickly from the other
room, her mother. She made a noise like some gigantic
beetle. *Hara-hara-hara.* The small one only wailed louder

and fell despairingly on her back. The mother lightly tapped her thigh. Tapped and tapped. The small one wailed and wailed. *Kora-kora-kora.* The small one's wail thinned, and it was plain that she was fighting something invisible stealing on her from inside. *Hara-hara-hara, kora-kora-kora.* The mother tapped and tapped. The taps grew lighter and lighter. The taps ceased. The mother threw a mosquito netting over the child's sleeping head.

First thing every morning the question was: Who might carry the baby? It was a tiny baby about three months old. There would be a great combat of words, then, always, and always as if the idea had come as a revelation, someone would say *Jong ken pon*—which means "Stone in paper" or "Stone paper scissors!"—and there would immediately ensue a dramatic matching of fist against open hand, one girl playing it with the next until the order of all eight had been determined. The mother quietly watched, then bound the infant to the successive backs, carried the cloth under the infant's arms, then crossed it once in front of the infant's chest, then around the child's chest, then two or three wrappings around the infant's buttocks and the child's belly, and finally one big knot. And off tramped the child, pleased, the infant seeming always to let its eyes lie still in its head so that the scene for it must have twisted dizzyingly with the twistings of the child who carried it. When the others tired of this game, there was one, always the same one, took on the burden. And whereas the others carried the baby for the sport and were soon bored, the one might carry it the rest of the day, carried it with the contented seriousness of a young mother. But her nose would run, and someone would point and say: "Worm, worm!" And each time she would slide out of the room and come back with a rubbed expression.

This is the kind of universal picture that makes one suspect that human civilization, though it is being subjected now to a severe shock, will not by any means be destroyed, shaken but not set back. It is the kind of picture that makes good men everywhere search with anxious eyes for the first light of peace, and perhaps gives to mankind greater hope of final permanent release from war than all the permanence that has and will be woven into the words of treaties.

I was writing while the children were playing. A page blew across the room. She who carried the baby, saw it, brought it back to me, and I could not for the moment remember with what words to thank her. Finally I found the syllables. All screamed with laughter at my pronunciation. Then suddenly the smallest, she who broke up the game, and who originally had fled at the sight of my horrible Western face, came over to me, my trouble with speech perhaps reminding her of her own recent trouble with speech, making me less strange. And she vent upon me an extraordinary flow. Suddenly she realized that I did not understand, and moved away, vaguely perplexed.

If an American has seven children in succession, all girls, he is apt to make a joke of it. Formerly it may have been a tragedy, but in this day the perpetuation of his family, his name, is not of much importance to him. He may want a boy to take over his business when he himself gets old. He may just like a boy around. But if girls insist on coming—well, they insist on coming. To the Japanese this is a tragedy. The Japanese wants boy-children. A girl-child is born in comparative quiet, but when a boy-child comes the whole family rejoices. And it is not, I think, that the father wants soldiers for the army—hardly any father anywhere really wants that. The nation wants that. In fact, in the exaltation of the boy-child there is, I believe, always the deep fear of losing it to the nation. And the fear is based on experience. The boy-child is kept in the fore of the daily life, but it is in the fore of the army, too. It may die early, a fact that everybody in the family constantly knows.

There is something else. The father of the seven would every now and then just touch the matter. He would begin: "The Japanese proverb is that girls break the house." That meant that the more girls the heavier the liability, because for each girl the father would have to find a dowry. Yet, if that were all there were to it, why did he go on having children? The coming of a son would not bring money into the house. Yet when I would say this to him he would seem not to understand. He would assure me that he would have more and more and more children, up to twelve, even if all twelve came girls, and more, till the strain ran pure boys. Someone had to have children nowadays! Someone had to make up for the families where there were only six and seven! At that he would laugh noisily. Was I then to think that all the last that he had said was humor? But then he added, carefully, casually, that the girls when they married went off to worship the gods of the husband's family. He would be sending seven worshippers to the gods of other families, and not one to provide for his own ancestors. At that he grew quite serious. He explained that it was not only a matter of giving one's ghosts pleasure, but of requiring them for the practical pursuit of one's daily life. A Japanese of this generation may not always exactly define these things to himself, though many would, and more would than ever admitted it to a Westerner.

But the father loved his girls also. He was watching them play. He shook his head. He told me a story of a man who, when he had three, and all three boys, complained bitterly that three were too many. Then came a fourth, a girl, but soon after she came she died. "Many a bad half hour has that man had from that day to this."

The children in that mountain house were well-behaved. A good way to see how Japanese children behave is to see them with Japanese-American children visiting Japan for the first time. The Japanese-American are so "bad" and free, the Japanese so "good" and suppressed. I remember particularly three Japanese-American who hated Japan with their whole souls, it restricted them so suffocatingly, and who every now and then, you could see, would feel suddenly frightened. The disciplining in that mountain house was inconspicuous, and not much of it. The fundamental disciplining being so inherent, periodic superficial disciplining was hardly necessary. The mother of the seven girls seldom disciplined them. Her way of doing it was to have the child stand up in one place for a time—would ask it to do that in a very low voice. The others never paid any attention to the one.

But the daughter-in-law with the single child had a different nature. She was a dusky stately lady. Her child would every now and then emit a cry of pain, a thin high-pitched tone that the child itself would immediately suppress. I would hear the cry, look quick, see nothing. Then, about the third day, I caught the daughter-in-law as she reached suddenly side-wise, pinched the child in the buttocks, and brought back her hand so fast it seemed on a spring. That was the punishment for some small disobedience. A pinch is such a concentrated silent method of offense. After that day I caught the daughter-in-law often. She appeared not to notice me. But the father of the seven girls did notice me, and slid over and carefully described how, if a Japanese child is especially bad, a bit of dry weed may be rolled into a cone and placed on the child's abdomen, and the weed set afire.

That daughter-in-law was remarkably soft-looking in that fog-soaked house. She wore a drooping edgeless kimono. There was never a new expression on her face. She had a languid way of moving. Nights when the mosquitoes came in—and they come by billions in July—she would set to work, noiselessly pitch the mosquito net tent, the *kaya*, that was as big as the room, light the incense that stood here and there in porcelain burners, and, her work done, drop like a heap of silk to the straw-matted floor, to fish mosquitoes out of the air. This last was a curious performance. She would reach, with unfailing skill would catch the mosquito between the tips of her pointed long fingers, then push it down into the red-hot charcoal. Mosquito after mosquito, night after night, always that skillful silent movement, and every mosquito singly executed. In intervals between mosquito catching she kept busy at some handiwork.

Then there was the unmarried daughter. She worked from early morning till late at night. It was a good kitchen, as such kitchens go, in spite of the rain was dry the whole time I was there. Strictly it was a narrow space beyond the edge of the room, bare earth with a well in it. Water could also be reached in from the outside by a bamboo pipe. The light was cellar-like. The cooking was on a charcoal burner set in the floor and near the kitchen, a moat around it filled with ashes to protect the house against fire. There were two sides to the burner, in the one the living coal, over the other always a huge steaming pot. Of me the unmarried daughter made nothing—not only did not understand me but did not care to try. I would want to get an egg boiled, would start to heat the water, a slow process, and she would need hot water and just take mine. Once I tried all day to get an egg boiled. Someone was forever at the business of fanning the charcoal to keep it aglow. The dishes had to be cooked one at a time, and were eaten as they were cooked, so that the meals were interminable. Of course there was rice. Several mornings a boy came up the mountain and brought small fish. And once there was chicken, a thin slice broiled on a sheet of steel that was laid over the charcoal. The rice was in a wooden pail with a wooden cover, to keep it warm. When you emptied your rice bowl you washed out the last kernels with tea, and the father of the seven told me earnestly that it was an immorality to do otherwise. There were many such small immoralities, this one on the basis of economy, but others not always so easy to explain. Hygiene was at the bottom of some. For instance, the father told me, one must not drink cold tea or eat in the open air, and when an English clergyman in Kagoshima ate a cookie in a rikisha half the congregation left the Episcopal church and joined the Methodist. The wasting of a single kernel of rice was in many houses held a great sin. When the mountain day was particularly foggy

and the moods particularly low, each would take his bowl
of rice to a separate spot of the room, eat it alone, and the
scattered collapsed bodies in that bad light were gloomy
to see. One or another might use his own small table, like
a sick-bed table, lacquered. Each had his own chopsticks,
that he washed in his tea. It was the unmarried daughter
who always murmured thanks at the beginning of a meal,
murmured thanks at the end, but the meal itself was eaten
even by the children largely in silence. In the speech of
Japanese women there seemed so often nothing positive.
The unmarried daughter in that kitchen worked also in
that covered way, did not show she worked.

The men of the family were middle-aged. They were on
a vacation, and therefore many hours of the day and night
they played a card game, an ordinary game rendered
always somewhat extraordinary by the quiet. The first
threw down a card, the second threw down a card, the third
threw down a card. Occasionally a shadow of cunning or
deviltry or jealousy would come into a face, but none of
them was ever agitated. Gambling in quiet is like drinking
whisky alone. The skinny boy did not play. The fog had
made him taciturn. And the father of the seven did not
play. He passed his time making small changes in the
house. One day he was putting a margin of glass above
the paper windows. He had a great deal of such glass. He
could not decide whether he should use green or white. He
asked me, talked it over with me fully. He chose green.

Another day he was hanging two specimens of writing on a bare wall. He would never have put that glass, or hung that writing on any wall in his house in the valley—but this was a summer house. He measured the wall in all directions with a meter stick. He changed the positions of the writings again and again. Once he said to himself: "Too high!" Once he said: "Too low!" The rest of the time he said nothing, worked with concentration, his movements quick and still.

Finally, there was the old woman. It was she did most of the talking, as in the house in Funakura. She would remember something the priest had said, and starting with that might go on for hours, and did not particularly need an audience. At home she lived in retirement, in the *inkyo*. That word means literally hiding-in-the-dark. When the young people take over the house, the old are retired to a small house to the rear. Their status is not left to chance, but prescribed. They are put out of the way of interfering in the lives of the young, but they are also not left to the whims of the young. This *inkyo* is apt to be tiny, two *tatami*, and placed as far as possible from the main house but still on the property. A Japanese described it to me as an old man's club, but it looked to me rather like an individual old man's home. The old were respected. If one went to visit the main house one stopped first at the *inkyo* and bowed, and perhaps left a bit of bean cake. A reward for old women who go to the *inkyo* is that they can smoke a pipe. Grandchildren are apt to visit on and off, knowing the weakness of the old for the very young, and beg a few *sen*. Important family conferences may be held in the *inkyo*. If a child is to be punished with the burning weed, that ceremony is almost sure to occur in the *inkyo*. And the very serious decision of a betrothal is settled there. The Grandmother at Funakura had been a widow many years, but no *inkyo* for her—she left it to her paralytic daughter. She said the *inkyo* was a place for whispered prayers and preparation for death, and that it was her opinion that religion ought to run through one's life and not wait till one was retired.

I have often thought that if I had to be anyone in Japan I should prefer to be an old woman, for the old women have the power—iron hand over the wives of the sons, iron hand over the daughters, the sons coming for advice on the smallest matters, the whole neighborhood coming for advice. Should this year's crop of rice be eaten, or stored against a better market, or sent to Nagoya, or used to brew *sake*. The old woman there on the mountain would go out-of-doors a moment each time the rain stopped, and she looked and walked like a wrinkled queen. Her breasts from many babies were stretched down to her waist, and I have been told that a woman may throw her long breast up over her shoulder, to nurse the baby that is strapped to her back.

What an essentially unrelenting pyramid such a family

is. The disciplined children below. Over them the disciplined mother. Over the mother the husband—son of the
house. Over the sons their dominant old mother. Millions
and millions of pyramids. What material for a fanatic
nationalism. What material for an army. Obedience is an
instinct. Submission is nature.

The boy who came up the mountain with the small fish,
also brought the newspaper. I could not read it, but I
would get my skinny friend to translate the headlines into
German, and where I was interested I would get him to
translate the article. That newspaper was all our contact
with the outside world. It was a poor way to read. But
there seemed to be so many articles bearing on a new
appropriation for the army, or a new ship launched, or
someone's opinion of Western civilization, that, added
to the taciturn family and the taciturn fog, I began to feel
I could not stand it up on that mountain much longer. For
me it was not a vacation.

Nights the bodies of the children would lie pell-mell in
the half-dark. One after another they would fall asleep.
She who always carried the baby looked in her sleep like
a Buddha. The mother of the seven would move from one
to the other, tuck the kimono around the legs, give the
kaya an occasional shake to shoo away any lingering mosquito, then herself disappear for the night. Her husband
would watch her, presently decide he would disappear
also. Without a word, without a nod, he would draw away

from the daughter who had stayed up to fan him. For a time after he had gone the fan continued its big free movements, only gradually, like some mechanic thing, came to rest. Me they would put up for the night in one of those portable rooms with oil-paper walls. I would snuff my light, and each time the act would blow a sudden life into the adjoining space, the silhouettes by turn be large and small, gray and black, soft and fantastic, till they there also snuffed their lights.

CHAPTER TWENTY-THREE
Two Stories

I HEARD TWO STORIES IN THAT FOG-GIRT HOUSE, BOTH told by the old woman.

A Buddhist priest was walking from his monastery in the Kirishima hills down toward the valley. He walked longer than he meant, darkness overtook him and he had to stay the night in the valley, so he stopped at a small lodging. The lodging keeper, a woman, old, led him up to the second floor, for the house had a second floor, and pitched the *kaya*. The priest fell asleep, abruptly waked, and saw a lovely girl inside the *kaya*. He rose to a sitting position. She moved backward. He stood up. She continued to move backward. She did not lift the *kaya* to pass out under it, but seemed to dissolve right through it, thence on to the oil-paper wall, to dissolve right through that also. Disappeared. In excitement the priest hurried downstairs to wake the woman. He need not. She was waiting for him. She said: "I know. Every night for twenty years that same child has come, stood itself inside the *kaya*, slowly disappeared. Twenty years. Every night. When she was alive she was the daughter of the other wife, the wife by law, and every day that other wife sent that daughter to call on her 'other mother,' her childless unmarried mother, to bid that childless unmarried mother good morrow. Every day. I strangled her." Said the Buddhist priest to the woman: "There are two ways of expiation, one active, one passive. The passive is the way of suffering. You have suffered. Henceforth look from suffering to the Buddha." The ghost returned no more.

That was the one story. A curiosity about this kind of subject is human, not national, and it is a curiosity always half-ashamed. Someone in the fog-girt house mentioned the strange phenomenon where the approach of death lays such a heaviness over the watchers by the bed that they cannot save themselves from sleep, and only when they sleep does the dying, who is using all his last strength to prevent precisely this, only then does he die. One in the house claimed she herself had had that experience. Another denied the likelihood. Another immediately broke in, said he had had the experience too.

This is the second story.

A servant crashed one of twelve precious plates. They had been in the family from the time of the Chinese Invasion. The master sent for the servant. She came onto the polished veranda. She bent her body low, till her forehead touched her knees. He pointed her into the room. Frightened, she slid in on all fours. He pointed her closer. Suddenly he grabbed from the tobacco *bon* the tongs with which they take up the hot charcoal, and with the tongs, one after another, plucked out the servant's finger-nails. On the tenth she died. The master shook himself. He had her body lugged away. Nothing more till night. Then it began to rain. It rained monotonously till midnight, when the oil by no human mouth was sucked from the lamp and the light went out, and the wood boarding of the house by no human hand was pushed aside, and from the dark night beyond there came a voice counting: One, two, three, four, five, six, seven, eight, nine, but instead of "ten" there was a shriek. That was all till the next rainy night, and on every rainy night it was the same. The master was a strong man, but the neighbors began to think that he grew strange. Stranger and stranger, till one twilight he burst into the house of the Buddhist priest. Words rushed from him. Said the priest: "On the next rainy night expect me." And on the next rainy night the priest came and at midnight, the voice: One, two, three, four, five, six, seven, eight, nine, but before the shriek could follow the priest broke in: "TEN!" And the ghost returned no more.

CHAPTER TWENTY-FOUR
Three Kinds of Constitution

A JAPANESE BRAGGED TO ME THAT JAPAN HAD WON its constitution without bloodshed. I asked him whether he thought that that was a good thing. He said, of course it was. He said, the constitution was just freely given to the people. I asked him if he did not think it was better for the people to get their constitution because they wanted it, because of something inside of them, some craving, some need. He said, oh no. He said, in Western countries the constitution was won at the end of a struggle between the powers and the people. But in Japan, on the contrary, "the constitution as the inviolable and imperishable code of basic laws was promulgated by the august and benevolent will of the Imperial ruler." I asked my question differently. Did he think that a plant grown in a hothouse and taken out into rough wet weather could be expected to have the vitality of one that had fought its way against earth, climate, and other plants, and had survived to a point of vigor? He said, oh yes. Then he said, there are three kinds of constitution, "the first has been brought into being by popular will as a sort of social contract, the second has been framed by mutual agreement and arrangement between the ruler and the ruled, and the third has been granted by the ruler. The first means denial of the sovereign power. The second means curbing the sovereign from exercising his power. The third is the one Japan possesses." I remarked that the Japanese constitution was frankly an imitation of Western constitutions, and did he not think that it would suffer from this. He said, oh no—coming late, it would not have so many mistakes.

The gentleman was an intelligent gentleman. He knew English fairly. He was a sensitive person humanly. But when he spoke of constitutional government he sounded centuries on the other side of Diderot, in fact, on the other side of Pericles. He was a child making big words with letters printed on wooden blocks.

CHAPTER TWENTY-FIVE
Marquis Ito, Democrat

I THINK IT MIGHT BE WISE TO LOOK AT A PORTRAIT OF the man who wrote the Japanese constitution. Hirobumi Ito. To keep the portrait in right perspective—and incidentally to get a side-glance on the working of one more Japanese mind, although a rare one—it ought to be steadily realized that this Japanese labored sincerely for peace, for negotiation instead of force, for the independence of Korea, and, by that, for the independence of Asia. Arguing with the War Ministry in 1905, Ito said: "I strongly believe that our whole system of military government in Manchuria must be abolished at once. When this has been done, Manchuria must revert to the civil rule of the Chinese, for the responsibilities involved . . . . are rightly China's . . . . The phrase 'the administration of Manchuria' has been in vogue among our people ever since the war, especially among our officials and even among our merchants and business men. Yet Manchuria is not a dependency of our country . . . . There is no justification for our exercising the rights of sovereignty within that sphere." I wish to emphasize by repeating, that this was early in the evolution of the new Japan, 1905, just after the peace following the Russo-Japanese War. If there was any man in the whole of Japanese history upon whom we would have been able to base a hope, it was Ito, and it remains a hope, possibly, that there was even once that kind of Japanese mentality.

Ito was born in the province of Choshu in 1841, twelve years before Perry's appearance in Yedo Bay. Choshu supplied much of the push for the new Japan. The way it is always stated, Satsuma created the navy, Choshu the army. A small spot on the map—the provinces of Satsuma, Choshu, Hizen, Tosa, and a few others—but with a pent-up hell that presaged trouble for the whole world.

Like Saigo, Ito was a poor man's son, though a samurai's, looked often up at the castle on the hill above his town, early felt his power, felt his clan's power, hated the Shogun, made his oath to restore the Emperor practically as soon as he could shape the words. His first school was in the coast town of Hagi. The teacher there divided the pupils into two groups, in each group put five who were outstanding, then set the two groups against each other, and since being numbskull was a mortal disgrace, learning was pursued savagely. After school the boys played war. One day Ito was general. His strategy

was first to drive his enemy into an area of dry weeds,
then in the weeds to continue the action, many small
encounters, the enemy kept occupied, he cautiously slipping off, coming back with fire in the form of a piece of
burning wood. He set fire to the weeds. Flames burst
everywhere. He routed the enemy, had the victory—and
could have burned his playmates to death. For this his
elders did not scold him as a dangerous wicked boy. They
praised him.

Like Saigo, too, young Ito made a pilgrimage to Yedo,
gossiped with his master, whose page he was, and in consequence got the chance to study in the so-called hero
school—a single small room known throughout the land.
It was not what we would think a school should be, but a
place where boys listened to the fervor of one who believed
in the warring virtues and in the exalted destiny of his
nation. It was atmospheric not curricular education. The
following gives an idea of the time and of the teacher—
when he heard of Satsuma preparing to fight the Shogun,
he rushed off to Yedo, to get in ahead of Satsuma, but
was discovered by the Shogun's police, questioned, tormented, convicted, escaped, then yielded up by his own
clan, and decapitated.

Ito with several others went to the prison to view the
body, collected the head, buried it. At about the same
time a Choshu nobleman endorsed the marriage of the
Shogun to the Emperor's sister—hideous appeasement!—

and his nephew, feeling he was compromised by the mere fact of being a nephew, committed suicide. This threw Ito into a rage, and he and other clan patriots hustled the uncle to prison and permitted him in turn to commit suicide. The patriots were not particular about whom they permitted to commit suicide, or whom they cut down, or what generally they did. The foreign missions, frightened by events, moved as far toward the sea as they could, Yokohama. Ito and his colleagues decided something ought to be burned. The buildings of the legations! The British legation, in Ito's opinion, was an ugly building anyway. So a conspiracy was formed. Each of twelve carried a package of explosives. They waited until night. They approached the building. They crept around it. Three hurled in their loads. Everybody else hurled in his. A guard rushed to the scene, but, as the story goes, when he saw Ito dancing with raised and shining sword in the light of the flames, he fled. It was at about this time also that the counsellor, pressed by the foreign missions into signing the post-Perry treaties, was assassinated. The counsellor who succeeded the counsellor was attacked, escaped with wounds, five of the six who attacked him were slain, the sixth, because he felt dishonored, wanted to commit suicide, but Ito argued with him, then left the room, came back to find the suicide gasping out his end. One after another the collaborators of the second counsellor were murdered. An historian was inclined to cast doubt on the unbroken continuity of the Imperial line—Ito assisted at his suicide. A supposed government spy was similarly effaced—Ito looked after this personally.

That is the way Japan was seventy years ago, and it ought to be a fact of interest to those who think assassination began with the Manchurian aggression in 1931, or that assassination is a recent method and not an almost fundamental one in Japanese government. And it is of interest that the future true democrat, Ito, could have lived such a bloody early manhood.

Abruptly now he got the idea that he ought to go to Europe, see how it went there, report back. He and four others forthwith cut off their samurai topknots, climbed up the side of a British ship, and when the captain hesitated, threatened convincingly to slay themselves at once in front of him. He smuggled them out to sea. Later, on the second leg of the journey, a captain played Ito a dirty trick. Though he had paid his passage, the captain deliberately misunderstood his scant English to mean that he wanted to be a sailor, put him to rough work, which he did against bad and prolonged fits of diarrhea. But that did not turn him against the West. Nothing turned him against the West. He saw passionately the importance of the West. In England he studied English aggressively. The weeks slid along. He went everywhere. He noted everything. Then, in a London newspaper, he read that Kagoshima had been bombed by the English, that

the *U. S. S. Pembroke* had been fired at in Shimonoseki
Straits, that the *U. S. S. Wyoming* had repaid the attack,
that more ships had been fired at, but that the Straits were
still not open, that the foreign powers were promising re-
prisal, that they were assembling their warships at Yokohama. Ito was in a frenzy. He could not possibly stay in
London. He must go back. He must go at once. Japan did
not understand. He would have to help everybody. That
was his work. Tremendous things were occurring inside
him. He went back. He had had some nasty experiences in
the West. He had spent eight months on seasick ships to
get five months of Europe, yet returned burning with enthusiasm for what he saw. He took the increasingly accepted view that to deal with the West, Japan must learn
how the West deals—with the difference that he practically alone caught the idea that Japan might deal by
diplomatic give-and-take.

The next months were intense. The time was near for
the powers to sail from Yokohama to the Straits. Ito
visited the British legation, convinced the Minister to
see him, argued him into delaying the attack for thirty
days. The Minister ordered a warship to take Ito somewhere near the Straits, and there drop him. With this
help, and with the help of a disguise, which he needed
because his hair had not yet grown back, he reached the
Lord of Choshu. He immediately gave him and everybody
around him a series of lectures. He explained to them the

world. He was even beginning to make them understand. But the time was too short. While he argued the ships of the powers had left Yokohama, were approaching the Straits. They made a formidable squadron. Nine British ships, four Dutch, three French, one American. Ito went out to them, was resolved to take on his own shoulders the problem of his ignorantly vain country. The shoulders were broad but not broad enough. The bombardment began. There was great damage. The Lord of Choshu learned some truths. Japan learned. Ito learned. It was he and one other who went with the white flag and brought about the cessation of hostilities.

In the course of these various activities he had several times fled from assassins. Once a maid hid him under a floor, squatted right over his head, saucily put off the assassins, all as in a Japanese play. Her captive was impressed. He married her the next year.

The Shogun died. A new Shogun came in. The rest we know—the end of the six and a half centuries was at hand, the Restoration was an accomplished fact. It happened that right at this time the future great port of Kobe was to be opened. The representatives of the legations were coming on invitation of the Shogun for a celebration. But the Shogun was no longer Shogun. The Imperial forces had been victorious, and the Imperial forces were, nominally, anti-foreign, and certainly the Japanese soul was anti-foreign. And an ugly thing took place—guns were fired into Kobe. That was serious. If a representative of the legations was injured or killed the warships of the powers would go further than they had the last time. It must be remembered, too, that the representatives were utterly bewildered. There was one person, Hirobumi Ito, whom they seemed to understand and who seemed to understand them. They held to him. He hurried to the Emperor—the Emperor Meiji—and made it clear to him that in the West when there was a transfer of power it was customary to assure the foreign legations they would enjoy the same protection under the new regime that they had under the old. The Emperor granted him the necessary authority. He hurried to Kobe —it was only a fishing village then—convinced the representatives of their security, averted national disaster. He was twenty-six, slight of body, a boy, and the most capable diplomat his country had.

Immediately he set about punishing the guilty. The person who had ordered the firing of the guns was permitted to commit suicide. To this function he invited the representatives of the legations. All but one declined. There was an attempted assassination of the English Minister. Ito had the "patriots" beheaded. Eleven French sailors were assassinated. Ito had eleven clansmen commit suicide. In this case he also prevailed upon the Emperor Meiji to apologize to the French. Assassinations were not doing very well. The number decreased.

The idea of popular government had been hinted at in the Emperor Meiji's first rescript. The nation was to have a constitution. No immediate steps were taken, so the newspapers, new in the land, began to agitate. Finally, in 1881, the constitution was definitely promised. It would be promulgated in 1890. Therefore, in February 1881, Ito was sent to Europe to study the constitutions of the principal European powers. He talked to Bismarck. He attended the coronation of Alexander III in St. Petersburg. His first impulses toward constitutional government he had had in England, but he based the Japanese constitution on the German model. He felt that that came closer to the country's traditions and needs. The later Emperors had been weak but the lords of the clans had often been strong and autocratic. Furthermore, there was a disposition to allegiance in Japanese nature, and if that could not fasten itself to the lords of the clans, it must to someone, and putting the Emperor into the constitution as the German type of autocrat seemed to take care of this.

He returned from Europe. For the formal drafting of the document he was to have several collaborators. A workroom was set aside in the palace.

There was always the greatest intimacy between Ito and the Emperor. The "sacred person" came and went in the workroom. There was eleven years difference between the two, Ito, of course, the older. There was a definite father-son feeling. The two talked in perfect frankness over every point of government. The older without any question influenced the younger in the direction of tolerance. There was steady trust. There was steady good humor.

The constitution called for an Upper House, a Lower House, a Premier, a Cabinet. That seemed to indicate a liberal document, but it was not. It could not have been. Japan had for a thousand years lived under a military tyranny, and a constitution was being dumped fully formed on the country, no time for growth, no time for evolution. If the new government was to have any chance at all it must not step off too far from the old. That, right or wrong, was Ito's belief. The constitution provided for the Privy Council, and, though not specifically written into the document, for the Elder Statesmen. The latter were a unique Japanese body, men who because of extraordinary performance to the country deserved special honor. The two bodies had no direct power, but, being the advisors to the Emperor, had enormous indirect power. Ito had brought from Europe also the hierarchy of ranks, Prince, Marquis, Count, Viscount, Baron.

The bad manners of the members of the two Houses in the early years was almost incredible. The confusion, the rancor, the corruption, the violence should have been anticipated, but they were not. Much of the time the meetings, especially of the Lower House, had something both of cruel farce and light opera. Indescribable bluster.

Indescribable disorder. I have visited a Japanese family soon after it moved from its uncomplicated Japanese dwelling into a complicated Western dwelling, and there was a parallel disorder. They who in their own were so very clean, became in our life dirty and helpless, and since they were active in their helplessness they looked frantic. The functioning of the new government looked frantic for the same reason.

The constitution was promulgated on February 11, 1889. The day was declared a national holiday. Since the Emperor out of his generosity—that was the theory—had bestowed the document upon the nation, the newspapers must accept it and not discuss it. Being Japanese, the newspapers believed this to be just. But that did not give them much to print, and it was an important occasion, so they used up their extra space and their always profuse inventiveness in maligning Ito. And he had, in fact, blundered. The promulgation did not occur on the exact date it should have according to the original agreement. This put the Emperor, who can make no mistakes, in the position of having made one, so his Minister was not only responsible but must be written down as a blundering old fool. Ito was President of the Privy Council. He resigned. The Emperor refused to accept the resignation. And that was the beginning of the farce, or, since human lives depend on the wisdom and the folly of a nation's officials, tragedy.

He came to be President of the Privy Council in the following way. One could not be President and Premier at the same time. His opponents did not want him to be Premier, so they recommended him for the Presidency, pretended they were honoring him while actually choking him—cut him off at the very time when he should have been and wanted to be interpreting the new constitution. The same expedient served again and again to keep him from using his power. He, of course, saw what was taking place, but it is the best evidence of his inherently democratic nature that he allowed it to take place. He let himself be played upon.

The constitution was vague on the responsibility of Premier and Cabinet. He said they were responsible not to the Lower House but to the Crown. That seemed from the outset to remove any chance of popular government, and if it did not mean that Ito was deliberately placing himself in the reactionary group, it must mean that he did not trust the people. How could he? They had never with any strength of voice asked for a constitution. When they got one they could hardly know what to do with it. They were more unprepared than the people of any large nation on earth. True, they were more intelligent than many, had great family discipline, and were democratic in the sense that person to person they regarded each other as fairly equal. But they had neither political experience nor tradition. To every one of us from our primers, the

whole long history of the West is a preparation for some
degree of self-government. The Japanese have been trying
to stand on our base without our heritage, and this has
made not only for the strain and awkwardness, but partly
for the violence, stubbornness, and vanity. They have, I
think, proved beyond question that our form of government is not for them, or not yet, and one of our mistakes
at the peace might well be an attempt to impose pre-
maturely upon them a form for which they have no instinct,
no wish, and no preparation.

The "party" groups were outraged by Ito's decision
regarding responsibility. The way they made their out-
rage speak was to accuse a close clansman of Ito's of corruption. Whereupon Ito went yet more reactionary—a
Japanese does not desert his family, and if it is not his
family that is in question, he does not desert his clan. He
took the premiership. The confusion went on. At the
opening of the parliament he was ill. His friend was to
read his speech, could not get it read because the parliament did not want to hear. The War Minister put in a big
budget. The parliament, thinking it was Ito's, or pretending to think it was Ito's, threw out the budget, then
decided on adjournment. Ito went to the Emperor. The
Emperor recalled the parliament. Ito hoped to remove
the disadvantageous treaty that his country had signed
with the Western countries. He did not immediately
succeed. There were anti-foreign riots. The parliament

wanted measures of revenge against the Western countries. Ito had the parliament dissolved. Another election. Another parliament. Another parliament dissolved. A newspaper expressed itself with freedom. The government closed the newspaper. It was all bad. Ito had written a constitution, the Emperor had promulgated it, the nation had had an election, and here was Ito bringing about one dissolution of parliament after another because parliament wanted to have its way. Stupid parliament, no doubt, but stupid parliaments have to be allowed to have their way, start the country to the devil, by their own folly bring on their own end, or there is no hope for constitutional government. A nation must submit to that kind of expensive learning. Japan never has.

The confusion went on—only not while there was war. As soon as the war with China broke out all heads came together and concentrated on that important one point. As soon as the war was over, the confusion began again. Ito had supported the war, but the generals had seemed to win the war. The populace went wild over the generals, heaped abuse on Ito, blamed him for how much everything was costing, for not keeping up the war until China was crushed and the whole of it annexed.

Meanwhile, through all this time, wherever there was the chance, his sincerity for peace was blandly employed as simply one more weapon by those who believed in war. They let him speak peace. They prepared for war. He

knew he was being used. But what could he do? He lulled
the outer world while the army built and drilled. To do
otherwise he would have had to love humanity more than
his own country—and there are few such men. And even
if he had been such a man, the method of proceeding is
unimaginable. The result was that his opponents could
never have invented anything like his peace propaganda,
because his propaganda was believed.

And the confusion went on. Ito offered the premiership to the War Minister. The War Minister passed it on
to a friend. But the War Minister needed money. So he
needed the Lower House. The Lower House was stubborn. The press joined in. The friend of the War Minister
resigned. The parliament was dissolved. Ito was asked to
form a Cabinet. The "party" groups opposed him. He
petitioned the Emperor. It was clear to him now that the
Cabinet must be responsible not to the Crown but to the
House. That is, he had changed his mind. To the truly
reactionary what he was suggesting was treason. It was
letting the state depend upon the will of the mob. It was
Ito violating his own constitution. All the powerful
reactionaries rose in anger. Ito resigned. He got the
premiership offered to a "party" group. It had no experience, nevertheless plunged in, blundered, was destroyed.
Bribery had its part in the destruction. Graft was in many
places. The country was changing from agriculture to
industry. Money was lumped in heretofore unheard-of

sums, to make the industries possible. The government bought, subsidized, borrowed, loaned, and this all was opportunity for graft. The War Minister got his budget by bribery, then deserted the bribed, filled the air with scandal. Ito again formed a Cabinet. He was accused of the bribery—but the Boxer Revolution broke out in China, and, instantly, bribers, bribed, Upper House, Lower House, Premier, Premier's enemies, Emperor, people, all put their heads together, concentrated on that important one point.

Ito again formed a Cabinet. This time it was sorely against his will. Things immediately went wrong. He resigned. He left for America, for New Haven, to receive the degree of Doctor of Laws at Yale at its 100th anniversary. Thence to France. Thence to Russia. Japanese political duplicity followed him. He thought that he was to arrange an alliance with Russia. He found that an alliance was in the process of being arranged with England. He favored an alliance with Russia. There was likelihood of war with Russia, and an alliance might stave off war. There was no likelihood of war with England, and an English alliance, while it would be a good thing, might positively encourage war with Russia—because the militarists in Japan would then be in no danger of England throwing her weight against them. So the war party had won.

The war with Russia followed. The fate of Korea was practically settled by the war. Ito nevertheless continued to work for Korean independence. He was offered the position of Resident General of Korea. He would be the first Resident General. He knew well the plan of his country, knew what its supposed destiny was, knew that there was nowhere among its leaders any moderation, yet accepted the role, though he could have had slight hope and must have gone to Korea in no happy frame of mind. His part was so ambiguous that it was tragic even before it led to tragedy. Russia was without a fleet, had been beaten in the war, was unsteadied by revolution, and Ito would have had his countrymen with him practically to a man had he snatched Korea, but he stood against his countrymen, and as for spheres of influence, was willing to divide equally with Russia. But Korea would be annexed. Everybody in Japan knew it. Everybody in Russia knew it. Everybody in Korea knew it. And into this atmosphere came the Resident General—lecturing for Korean peace and independence.

In July, 1907, the Emperor of Korea carried the case for his country to the Hague. The argument was that Japan had guaranteed Korean independence. She was violating it. The Japanese knew well that the powers would not dare side with Korea. Our own President, Theodore Roosevelt, said bluntly that the treaties would be ignored. Nevertheless the appeal to the Hague would give rise to international talk, therefore wiser to create a crisis in Korea, force the Emperor to abdicate, and then, of course, his representative at the Hague would have had the floor pulled from under him. Korean feelings rose. And naturally they were directed against Japan's mild-mannered, slow-spoken, Resident General. He seemed such an obvious villain.

Ito had gone home to Japan for a visit to his wife and son. He felt what was coming. On departing he practically took his final leave of them. He was extremely gentle to everyone. He admonished his son always to go through life with complete loyalty to the Emperor, regardless of the cost, because the country could advance and flower only as long as every Japanese did that. He reached Korea via the Straits, thence on to the half-Chinese half-Russian city of Harbin, now the principal city of Manchukuo. There he stepped from the train to review some Russian troops. A Korean walked up to him and shot him in the abdomen. The act was quiet and somehow, especially to those who were right there and saw it, incredible. Ito sank down, uttered: "The man is a fool." That at least was true. Thirty minutes later he died repeating a poem. He was sixty-nine. It has been hinted, though the cards were so stacked that that last detail would seem hardly to have been necessary, that the Japanese War Minister employed the particular assassin. Ito's body was brought back by train to Dairen, by battle-ship to Japan, and was given a state funeral. He was idealized, and his opponents helped in the idealizing, for they had now nothing to lose.

CHAPTER TWENTY-SIX
The Makurasaki Shop

Down by the sea some hours from Funakura is Makurasaki. That was the point of my next long stay. It was on my second visit to Japan. I lived in Makurasaki in the general shop.

The wares went right up to the edge of the shop on the street side. They made a kind of wall between the living room and the shop, and the kitchen and the shop. The entrance was a gangway between stacks of wares, where the customer was met, his clogs tucked under the floor, and, if he was a man or an old woman, his bamboo stick slipped into a vase. Then he was ushered in. He might stand as he bought, but usually he squatted, and the merchant went for the article and presented it in any position between standing and squatting, the position changing a number of times throughout the transaction. The least possible space was wasted either by customer or merchant, and in the early evening when business was at a height, there would be a long row of squatting customers, the merchants silently moving in and around one another, and in and around the customers, and in and around the wares.

Everything was sold. Silk, wholesale and retail. All variety of footgear. Straw hats. Umbrellas. Grills for frying fish. Other kitchen articles. Sewing necessaries.— many of them homemade. Tackle. Fish nets. Fish lines. Chopsticks. Whole cloth. Kimono. Cotton thread—nearly always white because there is nearly always enough white in the patterns. Bamboo products—water piping, sticks for fence posts, for chicken houses, for gates, kitchen utensils (handle and also the part usually made of metal), heavy sieves for separating gravel from rock, brooms (handle and bristle), shovels (handle and blade), trays also bamboo thread, bamboo fans, bamboo nails, straw overcoats, etc. What gave the shop its most characteristic look, however, was the china, literal walls of rice bowls, *sake* cups, tea cups, fish bowls, seaweed bowls, no expensive china, all for house use, strong browns, strong greens, strong reds, but not much red. The stacks left in one an uneasy feeling. As the merchants moved, the floor yielded and the stacks nodded. No one liked to talk of it, but there were sometimes strong winds from the sea, and there had been an earthquake, and there had been numerous typhoons. That china shop in a typhoon! They all remembered one typhoon that came without warning. The street was unsafe, so some forty neighbors took refuge in the shop. The shop was unsafe too, but it was the last place one could go. The whole house swayed. Everywhere wood rubbed creakingly on wood. It was bad. The children were frightened. But there was very little china lost.

Everybody in the shop sold. The old father, the mother, the son, his wife, his sister, and nights his married sister. The amount of work those people did, the length of hours, was incredible. They ate at separate times so that the shop could keep uninterruptedly going. The old father told me: "Quick eating, quick defecating, those together make one of the highest Japanese virtues." The shop was open before I rose in the morning, and kept open till the last customer, which might be midnight. At midnight the wife would blow out the American-type kerosene lamp, and the husband would pull around the slips of boarding that fit in the groove at the edge of the floor, with the usual thundering noise. This boarding was the sole barricade against assault of man, animal, and elements. The barricade was sufficient. At least so said the wife. She was the interesting one. Exceedingly tall for a Japanese woman, her height deliberately added to by her coiffure which was narrow at the temples and rose sheer over her head. A striking figure. She wore ginghams with bold patterns. She sewed all her own clothes and all her family's clothes. She knew the price of every one of the thousands of articles in the shop. She directed everybody's sales. She talked every minute of the day and night—and was eternally slipping over to one side to look

after a sick child. She had imagination for them all. She
had imagination also for me. I suggested hesitantly I would
like to eat eggs. There were no eggs. She announced my
need to one customer after another, and slowly, then
rapidly, then too rapidly, eggs came from near and far.
She could not understand how I could eat them soft-
boiled, but suppressed her point of view. And, of course,
I could not have eaten them fried, because there was no
frying pan and no butter. There was one stone step to
the kitchen, about eighteen inches from the floor to the
step, another eighteen inches to the slippery slabs that
covered the earth of the kitchen. I once saw the wife
come with a tray of teacups full of tea, and while stepping
up, with the free hand tie the sash around her kimono.
She was the kindest woman to her daughter-in-law—
would let her daughter-in-law go once every week back
to her own family to visit with her parents, and I do not
think this was because she thought her son responsible
for the child's illness. The child was a three-year-old girl,
lay always near a crack of street air, very pale, sick with
a degenerative disease, forever with its eyes was seeking
to follow the activity around it, would die in a year or two.
The labor of these people and the misfortune with the
child did, of course, not break them down. Quite the
reverse. It was the sturdiest family I was to see. They
have a saying: Rain makes earth harder.

CHAPTER TWENTY-SEVEN
"Knits the Raveled Sleeve "

I LAY AWAKE IN THE MAKURASAKI SHOP WITH THE sleeping bodies all around me, envied how still they were. We all slept at one end of the shop. Once I saw the old father light his long pipe, let the bowl rest on his hairy chest, fall asleep, no fear it would roll off and set fire to the straw floor.

The Japanese sleep easily. Whoever has traveled in the country will remember hot nights, trainfuls of sleeping bodies, one next another on the benches, feet folded under, jostling with the jostling coach, like rubber figures tacked down. On the crowded Beppu-Osaka boat—these were people on a pleasure trip—when night came everybody just lay down anywhere, on the floors, on the stairs, body next body, the choice places on the floors being reserved in advance.

Japanese life, unintentionally, teaches sleeping habits from the start. When a baby falls asleep on its mother's back the head drops where it drops, always looks as if it might break off or at least get out of joint, and the indifference of the parent to that bad position of the baby is, I suppose, an advantage later. On the mother's back the baby seems never to cry. The Japanese sleep with scant bedding, often just the bare floor, and no pillow, or one of those straw-filled bags that they say are so soft and that are so hard, or occasionally as in the old days a wooden pillow. They sleep often many together, which should get them used to sleeping quietly, and certainly gets them used to sleeping in spite of disturbance. One morning at about 2 A. M. I stepped off a train at a junction place, pushed open the door of the waiting room, and, almost literally, dropped back. A small-town waiting room. Every square foot of the place was covered with Japanese, tucked in, sleeping. I counted. One hundred and ninety-six. A crowded airless roomful of them, quietly sleeping. An American military observer says that during exhausting maneuvers the soldiers sometimes slept while walking. If there were anything I could at this moment give to my countrymen, besides more machinery for war swiftly produced, it would be just this capacity to sleep restfully whenever and however they had to. In that waiting room the sleeping mothers had their sleeping babies tied to their backs.

I once complained to a Japanese about my sleep. It was in a Tokyo restaurant, the customers eating here and there in groups on the floor. He said he would show me how to sleep, stretched full length, threw open his kimono, and rubbed his hand over his bare abdomen in circles, in the direction of the intestines—this, he said, was very important—and counted somnolently as he began each circle. So they do have sleeplessness. And of course their pharmacopoeia is full of narcotics. Then he insisted on me showing him how I would do it. I had to expose my bare Western abdomen. It was a fashionable restaurant, so nobody looked, but everybody saw.

In the Makurasaki shop eating, sanitation, business, and sleeping, everything took place in the one room. There was a diagonal runway, narrow enough to make it thrilling each time I crossed it, led to the toilet, that also managed to keep in the one room. This left still on the property a ridiculously tiny unroofed triangle, the garden. We slept, of course, with the light burning. They did everywhere. They put the oil lamp or candle in a pan of ash. The light was against thieves. Where there was electricity it was paid for according to the number of light sockets, so everybody just kept the lights burning all night. In fact, in the Makurasaki house there was no switch, and one could not have turned out the lights if one had wanted to.

CHAPTER TWENTY-EIGHT
The Makurasaki Theater

SEVERAL NIGHTS I WENT TO THE MAKURASAKI theater. You could work out the mind of a nation from its theater, especially an inflammable nation, that likes to be inflamed, that wants upwrought emotions, that trains them consciously. There are theaters of every size and quality. In that small-town Makurasaki theater they played a different play every night. The acting was often moving. The drama was almost all melodrama.

In the afternoon I had been walking on the seashore. A troop of boys blocked my passage. Two of them carried a drum and a third banged it while he yelled something wild and high. A fourth brought up with a banner. They were announcing that night's play.

It was announced again by a yet noisier troop that evening as I walked to the theater, about supper time. Hundreds followed this troop, though only a handful of the hundreds would be going into the theater. The boy who led the troop carried a pole with a huge head

at the top of it. The pole was heavy. The boy twirled the
pole back and forth in his hands, so that the head went
one way, then went the other, suddenly, with an extra
twirl, shot the pole swift and high into the air, caught
it behind him, twirled it behind him, again into the air,
caught it in front of him, then began tossing it from hand
to hand. The crowd gasped. The crowd yelled. The boy
was getting tired. And the next time the pole went into
the air another boy caught it, and manipulated it, so far
as I could see, as remarkably as the first. This all was to
the beating of drums that looked like frying pans with
long handles, half of them high-pitched, half of them
low-pitched, the rhythms strongly marked, and every age
playing the drums, one fat old barbaric female all energy
and breasts. The crowd did not only walk to the sides of
this procession, and follow it, but was anywhere in the
midst of it, so that for me the crowd was part of the
procession. One boy carried what looked like a giant
wedding cake, also on a pole, streamers from it, at intervals bells, and among the bells lights, some green, some
pink, one color burning at a time. The street got narrower.
The procession flattened itself against one side—was
giving room to two middle-aged men squatting in the
dirt, oblivious to everything, playing chess.

The street got wider again. It was now a small public
square. Around the edges of it were quill-shaped standards, at many angles, stuck carelessly into the ground

and moving somewhat in the wind, ideographs running up and down them, or here and there on them, or there might be only one ideograph. All were advertising the play, or advertising a geisha, or advertising an actor. There was a strong white light over the theater—it looked rather like the canvas front of a side show. On the rising ground to the right of the entrance was what you would have had to see twice to recognize, rows and rows of *geta*, hundreds of them, belonging to the patrons inside, each patron with a small wooden check tucked under his *obi* so as to get his own *geta* back. The admission ticket also was a wooden check. The audience was waiting. There were a few benches along each side wall, and a few at the back, but the large center of the open pit was just the floor with straw matting, divided by wood slats into various-sized spaces for the various-sized theatre parties. One man had a space all to himself and lay full length in it. The women squatted stiffly. The men wiped their faces and their necks with damp towels that they then laid across their shoulders. Meanwhile the children stole up along the low evergreen-edged stage and put their heads under the curtain to see what was going on behind—but immediately the heads came out again because at the back of the theater a sweetmeat vendor began to call. Soon there were three sweetmeat vendors. The first called, then the second, then the third, and each hung to his final vowel sound, sang it a while, with the voice of a crow. This tonal play naturally did not interest the children, who had the advantage of understanding the words. Somewhat later the children were eating, and later still, sleeping. Eating was the best part of the drama for them—seven hours of drama! One small boy said: he hoped they would just carry him home without waking him.

The curtain was a white sheet, a gift of a geisha to an actor, as was written in red ideographs across it. Behind that curtain was a second, gift of another geisha to another actor. A succession of curtains, advertisements for the geisha and for the actors. Each curtain was carried instead of pulled from one side to the other by black-kimonoed, black-hooded, black-masked supernumeraries, to an accompaniment of wooden clappers. A final curtain remained. Then the music began, two-stringed instruments, a *samisen* and a *koto,* joined after a while by several drums and a flute. Then once more the clappers, and this time the final curtain also was carried over, and that was the beginning of the first play.

The clappers, the musical instruments, especially the drums, were used throughout the play to step up the feelings—simple direct physiological stimuli. In the West we do that too, but depend much more upon the psychological stimuli. And I think it is quickly apparent that there is something noteworthy about a people whose musical accompaniment to the action of their drama is so often the flute and the drum. The acting was all in bold strokes. In this theatre men played the women's parts, a sixty-five-year-old man playing a young geisha—his makeup, his headdress, the forward inclination of his body, the patter of his clogs, and the mild snake-like movement that ran from head to feet, all sufficient, I believe, to give the males in the audience the proper masculine feelings. The fans of the actors were likewise used to step up the emotions, beating violently during the heat of a conference, standing still for a moment at the center of a thought, or deliberately by their lazy movement tantalizing—as a geisha an impatient suitor. The fans of the audience were apt to imitate the fans of the actors, indicating that the emotions were rightly transmitted. The Japanese in their homes always look somewhat like people on a stage, and I suppose it follows that the stage, that gets such training from the daily life, is easily realistic and strong.

There were three plays, many scenes, the action including bargaining, hoarding, saving, stealing, loving, hating, and then of course every variety of murder and suicide.

One play began with three men in a room smoking long silver pipes, periodically knocking off the ash, plotting. In the next scene one of the three slid into his sister's room. She tried to get him not to do the crime. He would not listen. In the next scene he did the crime, a theft. In the next scene, dark night on a dark road, the sister was pursued by the man her brother had robbed, defended

herself against him with a paper umbrella, a protracted
dance between them, he with his dagger, she with her
umbrella as a shield. You would think that must be absurd,
but it was not. Their fight whipped up to a frightening
intensity. Once the dagger and the umbrella changed
hands. Then changed hands again. The music meanwhile
was agitating the audience all it could. At last with a
scream the assailant cut a quick slit into the paper umbrella, and through the V thus created stabbed the woman
to death. As for the brother, he was made short work
of—someone stepping from behind a clump of bamboo
to finish him off.

The second play was a ghost story. The audience at
several points made the air whistle with excitement, but
never applauded. And the third play was a single scene
of *The Forty-seven Ronin*. It was after midnight by the
time that was over and everybody went home.

CHAPTER TWENTY-NINE
The Forty-seven Ronin

The Forty-seven Ronin IS A STORY, BUT THE FORTY-seven *ronin* were actual men. Their deed has had an immeasurable influence upon the Japanese mind. The graves of the forty-seven are in the grounds of the temple at Sendakuji in Tokyo. They have been there two hundred and forty years. Two hundred and forty years incense has been rising, people have left their visiting cards, have stood with bent heads. And it is all still very close to present-day Japan. I have seen Satsumans in an assembly room squat in a great square, small tables in front of them, read in turn the episodes—to foster the spirit of loyalty—this at eleven at night, all the faces fairly boiling with *sake*. Later I heard them go with loud voices into the night. The story has been told and retold. The story has been used by the greatest of painters and print makers. The figures of the characters have been baked into pottery. The songs of the various laments are a respectable part of Japanese music. The cinema has taken much of its substance from the story. Single episodes, or the whole sequence in one of its versions, is played on the stage of the capital and in every small village year after year, month after month. These are such favorites with the public that when it is necessary to revive interest in a theater, nothing will do as well as to announce that there is scheduled one act of *The Forty-seven Ronin*. Chikamatsu, who wrote one of the theater versions, is spoken of by the Japanese as their Shakespeare. He lacks the poetry of Shakespeare, certainly, but he has sometimes a bloodiness of imagination that Shakespeare either never attained or never employed. Murderers run through the episodes— strange murderers of such an extreme and, as it seems to us, pathological sensibility that they simply have to be rid of a certain person if they are to be able to continue to live on the earth, but once they have got rid of him they invariably themselves by their own hand choose also to leave the earth. It all helps us to realize on yet another side how far in the past the Japanese still are living, and why in war they may behave like men of some much earlier century. I have no doubt that many a soldier is carrying in his mind those old mediaeval images as he dives up into the clouds or down into the sea. "I am sixty-one," a Japanese said to me. "It is fifty years—I was a small boy when I saw the whole sequence of *The Forty-seven*. It took many nights. But there is still in me a most peculiar, a hot feeling, when I think of it. Of course, we often talked of the stories, and I read them again and again, and each time, no doubt, the old feeling was increased. It is that way with every Japanese."

What I saw that night at Makurasaki was one act of the theater version.

The story begins at the court of the Shogun. An envoy of the Emperor has announced his coming and must be received with impeccable feudal formality. Asano, a young lord, has been assigned to receive him. Asano is not experienced in the formality. So he turns for help to an older lord who is experienced, Moronawo. But Moronawo is a low venal person. And he is vain. He grows so insolent that Asano resolves not to bear it, draws his sword and strikes at him, would slay him if others did not intercede. Moronawo flees. Asano knows perfectly what he has done. To draw one's sword within the precincts of the Shogun's palace is punishable with (1) confiscation of one's property, (2) death, (3) a scattering of one's house. By evening of the same day he has already been informed of what is expected of him, and in the presence of his wife and friends and representatives of the Shogun he kills himself. Just before he dies his chief follower, Yuranoske, rushes in, laments, swears revenge. And later that night Yuranoske and many others bear the body of their lord away for burial, and all swear revenge. They will slay Moronawo. He has rendered them men without a lord, without a house, scattered like the waves, and the Japanese word for this is *ronin*. First hundreds ally themselves to the plot. But Yuranoske pretends to give up the idea of revenge, and many forsake him, but many remain loyal. Still he makes no move. More forsake him. Finally forty-seven remain. Moronawo, meanwhile, fully expects revenge, as he would have to in the kind of Japan he lives and conscious of the deed he did, and appoints spies who are to track the *ronin* and report on their behavior. This the *ronin* have anticipated. They go different ways. They lead lives that belie their intention. One sells bamboo in the streets of Tokyo. One serves as flunky in a palace. One is a beggar. The chief leaves his wife, lives with a whore, is perpetually drunk. That is his way of disguise. A Satsuman meets him, knocks him down, spits on him, accuses him of being a coward—later when he learns the truth commits suicide, and Satsumans brag of that one still. Not a leak in the secret, not in two years, not even when the mother of one of the men slays herself in his sight because of his laxness to revenge, hopes by her act to point out to her son his duty. Not a leak though forty-seven single individuals are involved. To the spies of Moronawo it seems that no revenge needs any longer to be anticipated. So the *ronin* get freer in their preparations. Bolder. They manage to place dependable persons right inside Moronawo's castle, to learn precisely his daily regimen. Finally, on a dark night, in the middle of a snow storm, they assault the castle, kill the guards. Moronawo flees to the servants' quarters, hides in the charcoal bin, but is dragged from there into the presence of all and hacked to death. They slice off his head. They march with the head to the graveyard of their lord, present the head to his spirit, thereupon give themselves up to the authorities and, one after another, forty-seven, kill themselves. They are buried in rows in front of their lord.

That is the story.

I asked for points in the story to be explained to me that night when I came back to the Makurasaki house from the Makurasaki theater. Soon everybody joined in the telling. The married sister, who had not said a word for three days, suddenly burst out in talk, corrected a detail. The wife corrected her, and the daughter-in-law grew excited and spontaneously recited lines—these women who forego outside events so entirely in their lives.

It is interesting to consider certain moments in the story, because they are so full of Japanese feeling and Japanese point of view, and because they make us better able to grasp what a tremendous quantity of training every Japanese has had in the honor-assassination-suicide complex. Frederick Dickins long ago translated into English a succession of the theater episodes.

One of the chief themes is loyalty. Loyalty is as strong or stronger to the dead than to the living. The dead seem often more alive than the living. Asano is ready to plunge the knife into himself. His beloved are around him grief-

stricken. But not one word of kindness does he speak to
them, does not seem in the least to think of his affections
at parting from the earth. Indeed, he seems already among
the dead. He is planning to get up first thing tomorrow
morning in the thick of the ghostly life, and have his
revenge. I take up at a point of his speech: ". . . An
inextinguishable rage fills me to the very marrow of my
bones. Like Masashige—who in his agony, still possessed
with an intense longing for vengeance upon his enemy,
swore that he would come to life again to have it—I, too,
living or dead, will have my revenge." He talks on. The
heat in him grows. The state of the dead becomes so
actual that one begins oneself to believe that he will
literally be able to cut through death, return, and take
his vengeance on the living.

Not just anyone has the right to die by his own hand.
It is a reward. It is a privilege that has to be earned. It
is an honor that has to be won. Kampei, one of the followers, is speaking. ". . . I was overwhelmed by the news
of our master's self-dispatch . . . and thinking that the
least I could do was to accompany my lord on the dark
path, I laid hand upon my sword when I was arrested by
the reflection that my lord would ask me what high deed
I had done to entitle me to follow him." In other words,
he has realized just in time that he has not the right to
die. He hangs his head in misery. There is nothing for
him to do but go on patiently living.

The ground on which a man and his ancestors have lived their lives is sacred ground. It contains more than their house, more than their own past, more than their own youth. It reaches back to earlier existences. It is shared with a whole train of ghostly ancestors. Hence the believability of the pathos of the *ronin* leaving the castle, so much greater than the pathos of leaving their wives and children, or this life. ". . . And rising to their feet, their hearts heavy with the thought that they were quitting forever the castle where for generations their ancestors, and where they themselves for so long a time had for night and day done their duty as samurai, the retainers of Asano slowly and reluctantly, and with many a wistful look back, passed out through the castle gate." It becomes a most moving point of the story, one that the Western mind also perceives. The feelings for the ancestral ground adhere everywhere like webs. Official Japan would sometimes quite willingly have been rid of them. Official Japan has always complained that the people would not go to the annexed territories. They wanted an empire but they wanted to stay at home. I doubt if that was ever the state of mind, for instance, of the English boy. He knew empire not as a wish only, but himself expected to go out. In the beginning it may not have been so natural as later, but there was certainly nothing deep and fundamental in him that he had to struggle against.

One kills oneself because there is a situation that calls

for suicide. One does not kill oneself to be rid of an unhappy life. Later in the story Kampei has killed himself,
his father-in-law has been murdered, his bride has been
sold to a geisha house. From our point of view Kampei's
mother-in-law would then have every reason to commit
suicide, but there is never the slightest question of her
doing it. She complains. She moans. In front of her lie
the two bodies, her husband's and the son-in-law's who
was to have supported her. The bloody knife lies there
too. But she will not take this escape from her agony.
"Is there anyone in the world so wretched as I? My husband murdered, my son-in-law, to whom I looked for support after my man's death, a corpse before my eyes, my
darling daughter separated from me, none but myself, a
poor old woman, left—why should I live all alone in the
world, what have I to hope for! O, Yoichibei, Yoichibei,
would I were with you!" Every Western tragedy would
end this scene with her immolation. Not a Japanese.
Suicide is the easiest thing in the world, but that mother-
in-law's situation is not one that calls for suicide. She
simply has not yet the right reason to put an end to her
life.

Cruelty is not unnatural. Cruelty is not the sign of an
ignoble mind. Yuranoske, the chief, has a truly noble
mind, according to the Japanese, and according to us on
most counts. And Kudaiu is just a miserable spy. Kudaiu
is hiding under the floor. Yuranoske stabs him through

a crack, then drags him into view. He is not dead. Yura-noske taunts him by recounting all the details of the plot he came to discover. In the room with them are a geisha and her brother. Yuranoske now commands the brother to cut Kudaiu to pieces. No one shrinks in the slightest from the prolonged torment that follows. After a period of hacking they change the plan, decide that it will after all be inconvenient to have Kudaiu die in the room, so drag the living body off onto the road to finish it there. (They even learn from such hacking lessons in hacking. The younger samurai used to perfect his swordsmanship on the bodies of criminals, studied the vulnerable spots and the special thrusts.) What makes Yuranoske's conduct particularly difficult for us to understand is his place in Japanese history, perhaps their most ideal hero, the pure knight avenging wrong.

A commoner has not the right to follow his lord to the dark world. He would have to be a samurai. This makes one poor commoner most wretched. He laments his state. He begs one who is presently to die to carry a message to one already dead from one who has not the privilege to die. "At least, when in attendance upon our lord upon the dark path, you will not fail to let him know how gladly I would have accompanied you. . . ." His speech goes on to tell us that the luckier ones, who in a short while were themselves to die, deeply moved by his earnest words, burst into tears and ground their teeth in sympathetic rage, as they saw how bitter was his distress at finding himself unable to give full vent to his loyalty—to die, in brief.

The sister-brother relation has extraordinary possibilities. A brother is here speaking to his sister. She has accidentally read a letter that was meant only for the eyes of the chief. The brother is wanting to become one of the *ronin*. Soon his speaking has turned to pleading. "The letter you read contained matter of great importance, and it is quite clear that the chief only wanted to get hold of you to put you to death, and so keep his secret. You know the proverb, 'Walls have ears.' If his designs were to get wind, even if not through you, your fault would be still as great. You have read a secret letter and cannot escape the fate. Better to die by my hand than by that of some other man—and if I slay you and tell our chief that, though you were my sister, I could not pardon you, as knowing what ought not to be trusted to a woman, he will let me add my name to the list of the conspirators, and I shall share with him the glory of the enterprise." And the Japanese mind apparently extols the beauty of his amazing intention.

Finally the story reaches the point where the *ronin* break into the grounds of Moronawo's castle. The commotion is so great that the neighbors come to see what is happening. "On either side, the roofs of the buildings were crowded with men carrying lanterns, twinkling in the darkness of the night like stars in the heavens." Quickly Yuranoske steps forward to explain. He apologizes for making a noise so late at night. "We are the liegemen of Asano. Some forty of us are banded together to revenge our lord's death upon his enemy, and we are now struggling to get at him. We are not rising against the government, still less have we any quarrel with your lords. As to fire, strict orders have been given to be careful, and we beg you not to be under any apprehension on that score. We only ask you to leave us alone, and not to interfere with us." The neighbors instantly enter into the spirit of the situation, do not for a moment consider preventing the assassination of the man who lives next door, but courteously state their complete approval, and turn back into their houses to continue their night's sleep.

CHAPTER THIRTY
Matsue Suma

WE THINK MOSTLY OF THE ACTORS OF JAPAN. There have been actresses of great note. The following was told me that night when I got back to the Makurasaki house from the Makurasaki theater.

At sixteen Matsue Suma came to Tokyo from Nagoya. She applied to enter the drama school, but could not be admitted because she did not have a middle school education—no English, and what can one do without English! She begged. She was refused. Finally she asked merely to be allowed to sit there. To be rid of her they let her sit. Secretly she married—married a normal school teacher. Then began to quiz him, night after night after night, drew an education out of him, till he rebelled. She went on without troubling him, was admitted to the drama school, graduated from the drama school—some say it was by sacrificing her chastity. She went on sacrificing. Her husband divorced her. At last she got her chance, in Tolstoy's *Resurrection*, and was overnight the most known of all the actresses of the modern school. Then *Romeo and Juliet*. Her name on every tongue. Eulogies. There were thousands of poems to her. Next she fell in love with a dramatist, a violent affair, a married man. He died. On the seventh day after his death she decided to follow him. And as there had been thousands of eulogies, now there were thousands of laments.

After they had told me the story one after another in the room said: "When will there come another Matsue Suma?"

CHAPTER THIRTY-ONE
Assassination

ASSASSINATION IS MUCH THE SUBJECT OF THEIR drama—and of their life. Yet the many assassinations of the last ten years could lead us to wrong conclusions. We could, for instance, too uncritically accept that a small clique had terrorized the nation, grabbed the power, imprisoned the Emperor in flowers and silk, and that the nation was actually against the clique. That is, we could too completely believe the thesis that it is a particular gang that has precipitated the country into war. There is a gang, no doubt, but if it were not this gang it would be another—gang rule is the way Japan has functioned right through its history.

Possibly, too, the enemy gang idea may seem necessary to us for propaganda purposes during the war. It ought not to be. I admit that a bogey is a simpler fact to face than a nation—a small group of bad men, black sheep different from the run of the flock. It is simpler to hate a gang than a people, which we might otherwise think we would have to do. Whether we believe it is a gang or do not believe it is a gang, is not apt too much to affect the course of the war, except that it is wise as far as possible always to know your enemy for just what he is. But at the peace—when we hope to have militarily annihilated Japan—we certainly would deal one way if we were dealing with a gang, and another if we were dealing with an entire people. A gang would be easy to liquidate. It would not be easy to lop off at a stroke a nation's history and psychology, though I am not denying it would accomplish something to get rid of the chief exponents of that bad history and psychology. However, we partly failed in the last war exactly because we saw the bogeys, the Kaiser and the other absolute monarchs, dramatically tumble, with a quick substitution of republican government that we thought must be like our own. The Kaiser was the gang. He abdicated, and we thought, and certainly can be forgiven for wanting to think after four years of bloody war, that all was well. We can finish a gang with a death sentence. But a nation of 100,000,000 we would have somehow to convince, and it could only be slowly. There is the danger that we shall be tired by the end of the war and that to settle with a gang may be a tempting invitation carefully to be avoided. For myself, I would not know where in Japan the clique of bad men ended and the nation of good men began.

At least, assassination and general violence in public

life strikes the plain people of Japan with less astonishment
than it would us. After the mass assassinations on February 26, 1936, I received a letter from a Japanese novelist
in Paris. In the course of the letter, on an altogether
different subject, she lightly dropped these sentences.
"What did you think of the Japanese events of February
26? Such a perfect performance. My husband wanted to
burn incense sticks to the rebels and scolded me because
I had no more left. Meantime I received such a cute letter
from my mother who, with my sister, passed through the
events with perfect composure and a kind of out-of-touch
attitude." That is how an intelligent and talented modern
Japanese woman, and one who, besides, was living far
away in a Western democracy, could pass off assassinations
that removed a half dozen of the leading men of the
nation. There are some fundamental reasons for that.

In the first place it appears that death is not as important
in Japan as it is with us. It was not in the old Japan. It
was not in Lafcadio Hearn's Japan. It did not seem to
me to be in the liberal Japan of the twenties. And it does
not seem to me to be in present Japan. Religion is a part
of that. The philosophy of science has made less inroad
in Japan. I was always brought up afresh with the paradox
of an apparently modern Japanese in Western clothes
and a Western type of education, often a doctor of medicine, saying flatly that a man stepped off from the present
life into the future life just as he had stepped from the

past life into the present life. Past, present, future, were one. You came. You were. You went. As a contemporary Tokyo merchant put it: "The present and the past are one and the same, and so are the present and future too. . . . A Japanese thinks that while his death is the end of his life in this world, it is also his return to the past. After death he will go to the country of the gods, who are his ancestors. . . . The dead go to the country of the gods where their ancestors live together." The man who spoke these sentences is by no means a child in practical affairs, has earned millions of *yen*, has played in politics, has traveled around the world. To him personally death did actually seem an indifferent matter.

The nation, on the contrary, is to the Japanese not an indifferent matter. For the nation he lives and dies with strongest feelings. He acts on these feelings with selflessness and recklessness. And if you sacrifice your own life lightly for an end in which you believe, you are apt not to take too seriously sacrificing your neighbor's life for that end. Now add that arbitration is not an especially Japanese way of arriving at conclusions, and assassination becomes at least a more natural political measure in Japan than it would be in any other country of the modern world.

Even the reader of these not very historical pages must realize that assassination did not begin, for instance, in 1931. It was altogether honorable for the samurai of the old days to assassinate if that was useful to his family or his clan, and today it is honorable to assassinate for the sake of that union of the clans called the nation. In the years right after the Restoration any foreign minister or foreign statesman was regarded as legitimate subject for murder—the British Minister almost lost his life on his first audience with the Emperor Meiji. Okubo in 1877, when he got word of the Rebellion, thought first of assassinating Saigo as the way of meeting the difficulty. Saigo escaped, to kill himself. Okubo was assassinated the next year. In 1889 Mori, Minister of Education, was assassinated on the day of the promulgation of the Constitution, because he was progressive. Ito was assassinated by a Korean, but the very highest of Japanese drove him into the corner where the assassin must inevitably reach him. The first commoner to rise to the premiership, who made it look as if party government finally would have its chance, was removed by assassination, and party government never has had a chance. Hara's assassination was in the liberal twenties. Yasuda, founder of Yasuda Financial House, was assassinated the same year. The number of assassinations before 1931, in fact, is legion. Assassination is an old, deep-rooted, dynamic method in Japanese public life, and difficult to dig out, if indeed there has ever been much will to dig it out.

I asked an intelligent Japanese to explain to me about assassination. "It is like voting," calmly came the answer that almost knocked me down. He went on. "Things get settled. The people get too much of something and someone is assassinated. And what you call the brains of the gang, they are sometimes the mildest men—you know that. The army is on top now, but the time will come when that will end too—by assassination."

And assassinations have shown themselves quite capable of accomplishing results. They have been a useful instrument—for the Japanese naturally must think that whatever has brought the nation to its present point has been useful. Okubo's assassination, for instance, forced the government to heed the popular cry for local assemblies. Okuma's attempted assassination hastened the removal of the immunity of foreigners to Japanese law. Premier Hamaguchi pushed through the ratification of the London Naval Treaty in 1930. The naval staff was demanding equality with Britain and the United States in the number of warships, had Togo on its side, and only with great difficulty and only nominally lured him away. The Navy had never been opposed since the great victory of Tsushima. Now it was. The treaty thus was ratified by the Emperor at the advice of the civilian head of the state. Hamaguchi, accordingly, was shot in Tokyo Station, and died the next year in consequence of his wounds. There would never again be an agreement to an inferior naval ratio.

The assassinations since 1931 have been more conspicuous partly because the country has been going ruthlessly to an end that seriously concerns the Western world. Their list is without doubt formidable.

Inouye, President of the Bank of Nippon, Japanese Finance Minister, with the habit of figures, therefore conservative, therefore not free with public money, was assassinated. This was in February, 1932. Money became freer.

Baron Dan, head of *Mitsui*, business man, therefore conservative, was assassinated March 5, 1932. "By a reactionary young man." Business began to make sacrifices to the army.

Inukai, 30th Premier, an old man, therefore conservative, was assassinated in the coup of May 15, 1932. "By fanatic naval officers." Young naval officers, and the impression was that they were allowed by their superiors to be fanatic. Youth and fanaticism gained ground.

Araki, the bellowing extremist, had talked himself out of the War Ministry. Mazaki belonged to his group. Hayashi succeeded Araki to the War Ministry, dismissed Mazaki, whereupon an excellent swordsman of the group walked into the office of Hayashi's first assistant, and cut him down. It was a warning. The warning was heeded. The extremists gained ground.

In the assassinations of February 26, 1936, a great number were involved in the plot, and managed a successful secrecy that makes you think of the Forty-seven. Not a leak, though many single individuals were involved. The assassinations took place at numerous points around Tokyo, and the Japanese were good as usual at timing treachery. The assassins accounted for Takahashi, the aged finance minister, Viscount Saito, Viscountess Saito, General Watanabe, Admiral Suzuki, and many of those who were on guard around them. The Premier, Okada, hid among his servants, like Moronawo when the Forty-seven finally beat into his castle, and escaped by being a mourner at his own funeral. Something was here again accomplished. The army leaders agreed to get rid of the extremist element, which they never permanently did, and the civilian leaders agreed to supply more money for the army, which they did.

Assassins, finally, have always had honor in Japan. The country abounds in monuments to them through the generations. Their trials have been a forum for the dramatizing of clan or national patriotism. The trial of the assassins of the February 26 outbreak was said to have been secret because assassination was becoming too alluring even for the Japanese—or, it may be, there was a fear that the warm-blooded might speak out of turn to the world of Japan's plans for the conquest of Asia, that were to take a violent step forward the following year.

CHAPTER THIRTY-TWO
They Take Their Games Seriously

THOSE TWO CHESS PLAYERS IN THE STREET THAT LED to the Makurasaki theater played there every night, I found, interrupted traffic every night. No one objected. In the Makurasaki shop there was always so much to do that there was no time for games, and, in fact, no space to play them. Everywhere else they were important. The Japanese take their games seriously. The feeling always left upon me as I watched them was that they did not merely play—they trained.

They play our chess. They play Japanese chess, not too different from ours, but on a board with 81 instead of 64 squares. They play checkers. They play *goban*, which is not *go*. They are proud of playing *go*. It is played with 180 white and 181 black stones, and played on a board that has 361 intersections. A ship captain at Makurasaki talked to me at some length about *go*, said it was much more difficult than chess, that Americans and Europeans never learned to play it, and I had the impression that it satisfied something in him to play a game that the white man could not easily, that he liked disciplining himself at such a game. Yamamoto, the Commander-in-Chief of the combined Japanese fleet, is said to be the champion *go* player of the Navy.

I played frequently with a Japanese whose excitement was the inverse of his talent, and for all the kinds of game he played, billiards, American cards, ping-pong, and handball. We were thrown closely together over a period of six weeks. I have no interest in cards, but it was always much easier to play with him than to escape. He seldom won, yet his enthusiasm kept up. He was a poor and careful man, yet he would play for money, sometimes have a bit of preliminary argument with himself, and yield to his worst nature. He glowed increasingly as he played but he did not talk. Concentration of players is respected. To us such behavior seems humorless. No one at a wrestling match ever creates disturbances, and both baseball and tennis are followed by the crowd with a patient quiet. I remember two brothers who played together a variety of games—but during the games they were never brothers. Grandmother's husband, the man of the two *tatami*, used to say that one must so concentrate that if a messenger were to come into the room while one was playing one could look up casually and say: "Oh, did my father die?" He also said that the hollow on the bottom of the old *go* boards symbolized the fact that one was justified, if a man disturbed one's game, to cut off his head and stand it up in that hollow.

I played poker nights in the small dining room of the *Kaga Maru*, the green cloths on the table tops, all but one light economically turned off, the sea and the wind close around the ship. There were the captain, the purser, the chief engineer, one or another of the mates. They would relax just enough to let me count in Japanese, or use a Japanese expletive, because that was really all I could do—so that the game should amuse me too. The game would go on as long as I could keep awake. The captain would have some trouble maintaining his captainly urbanity, but he would maintain it. It was an odd feeling to be out at sea in that stage-lighted small box, gambling. The intensity was painful. They were sailors and of course did not know when the ship rolled, but every so often it would lurch, and pitch all the cards and chips in one moment off the table, and with great earnest the crew would recover the pieces out of the shadows, the urbane captain also getting down on his belly.

There was a Chinese first-class passenger, a boy, the only Chinese on the ship, played shuffle-board with the Japanese, and was a great torment to them. He had two vices: one, he played indifferently, and two, he did not think it wicked to cheat. It is difficult to cheat at shuffle-board, but he managed it, constantly, was so frank about it that any national but a Japanese, or perhaps a German, would have been amused. The ship's crew could not refrain, one after another, from pointing the cheating out to me, on the chance I did not see it. When the crew played against each other there was something definitely savage about the violence, the way each tore into his opponent, his face aglow, the gloating, and the players would often combine an accuracy of shot with a boyish casualness to a point almost frightful, like any raw natural phenomenon. There was one Japanese officer would dance about after a victory, grin, rub his abdomen like a satisfied baby, then dash off. "I must go now to the bridge, watch till seven-thirty, but then will be back to play after supper." He would scream the words over his shoulder to his victim.

In New York the bacteriologist, Noguchi, and the photographer, Hori, played chess. In the beginning Noguchi was able to play only American chess, then his friend, Hori, taught him Japanese chess, and he played now with great persistence—almost but not quite letting it interfere with his real work. He played to win—they all do. And winning, for his kind of temperament, depended on such rapid playing that the enemy got confused. Therefore he had unanswerable arguments for the stupidity of a slow game, and for the intelligence of many games, victory being in the greatest number of games won. If you played enough games you could sacrifice a few. His wife, a Western woman, told how she would hear the chess men crack against the chess board, louder and louder, till she

would call from the bedroom and tell him to come to bed,
and immediately the cracking would die way down, then
gradually and helplessly rise again, and this sequence
happened over and over. Suddenly, though he had acted
all the while as if he had absolutely no interest in the
number of games won, he would rise from the table, push
away from it, remark that he must stop for the night,
remark also that he had won, not make too much of that,
light a cigar, be pleased and vain. If perchance a night
intervened in which he did not win, he was there the very
next night to renew the play, whereas if he won he might
not be around for weeks.

The game interest goes out into everything. There was
a famous Tokyo gang of thieves. The chief of the gang
wanted a valuable tobacco pouch owned by a citizen of
Nagoya. The citizen always wore the pouch next his abdomen under his *obi*, difficult to get at. The chief sent his
men, one after another, the clumsiest first, finally went
himself. And came back with the pouch. They asked him
how he did it. "Bought it for an absurdly high price—and
stole back the money." This last type of game might be
played at a peace table, I suppose.

CHAPTER THIRTY-THREE
Hara-kiri

Hara-kiri and assassination, as I have suggested, are generally closely related, breed each other, and in peace-time help to keep up the tensions of war. The Japanese have sometimes committed hara-kiri so lightly it is a mystery to the Western mind. A Satsuman, twenty-four years old, had a conviction as to government policy, bore the document stating the conviction to the Emperor, presented it, and in order to impress the importance of it, there and then committed hara-kiri.

The word hara-kiri means belly-cutting. It was the samurai's favorite method of committing suicide. He began training for it from when he was young, and it was his hope through life, if the hour came, to enact it with courage. Hara-kiri might be voluntary or involuntary. If the samurai was condemned to death he considered it a privilege to be allowed to perform the sentence on himself, for it was a disgrace to die by the executioner's hand. And if he was dying for some reason of his own, some breach of honor, he regarded drowning, poisoning, hanging, leaping into a volcano, as methods to be left to the commoner, not worthy of the samurai. They are still so regarded. To us his reason might often seem insufficient. For instance, the samurai was supposed never to break his word. When he borrowed money he gave no note, just promised to pay back on a certain day, and was not apt to break his promise, but if he did he performed hara-kiri for the disgrace. A Japanese acquaintance of mine writes as follows. "With regard to hara-kiri, most foreigners have more or less knowledge of this method. . . . The subject ends his life by cutting open his belly with a dagger. In order to accelerate death, in later times, it has become usual for a friend to stand behind the chief actor in the tragedy and to chop off his head when the latter thrusts his dirk into himself. . . . It requires great courage. . . . Barbarous as this method of self-destruction may sound to foreign ears, the fact that it has been in long practice shows how readily and with what composure Japanese well-bred in the spirit of Japan face death. . . ." The farmer was not allowed the privilege of hara-kiri. Women usually have not cut open their abdomens but the arteries of their necks. An occasional woman has done so for the remarkable reason of making plain to her husband that he has not behaved properly—for instance, has not been loyal to a friend.

It is estimated that for centuries there were at least 1500 hara-kiri per year. Nowaday the Japanese apparently do not commit suicide any more than other peoples. Modern suicide statistics do not place Japan in the highest rank. The rate per 100,000 is higher than in the United States, but considerably lower than in Austria. In the Irish Free State it is lowest of all, meaning that the Irishman has greater courage to live, or that his lucid mind will not let him take events that personally, or that what drives others to suicide drives him to drink and laughter. His kind of superstition also plays a part in preventing him. The Japanese kind does not.

I know, of course, that classical hara-kiri is not common in contemporary Japan, but the Japanese is interested in the whole idea of it, knows every detail of the ritual. He likes to talk about it. He likes to read of it in the newspaper. He likes to see it on the stage. In the village theaters one is never able to avoid it.

On that morning of my first arrival in Japan the doctors took me from Yokohama to Tokyo, dropped me at the Imperial Hotel. Later one of them came to my room, informed me about the trouble at the American Embassy, and another informed me that six Japanese had committed hara-kiri in protest to the Exclusion Act and that their bodies had been left on the sidewalk in front of the Embassy. Of course, there were no bodies in front of the Embassy. I went to look. But the fact that even a doctor might paint that particular picture speaks for itself. Several times a doctor would be showing me the countryside, he and I would come on a waterfalls, and I involuntarily start to admire it and he stop me with some remark like, "What a place to drop down!" There are waterfalls everywhere famous for their suicides. A dozen Japanese will inquire of you earnestly if you have been to Mihara, the island volcano, where every year hundreds end their lives. We Americans may gossip over why someone was driven to suicide, but we do not have an excited and almost happy interest in the process. The Japanese does. When I remarked to a Japanese that the man who commits hara-kiri is after all dead, the Japanese, a university man, blurted out protestingly "No, that's where his life begins!"

There are reasons for the Japanese interest in hara-kiri. History is part of them.

Lafcadio Hearn relates how in the earliest times the retainers of a lord let themselves be buried in a ring around the body of their master—up to their necks so that they died sometimes of thirst, I suppose, and sometimes because creatures came and ate at them. Wives also followed their husbands. That is, the servants and the wife followed the master.

The national religions, ancient Shinto and the Buddhism that came in later, both made suicide easy psychologically. Shinto with its strong emphasis on a man's coming from the ghosts of his family and returning to the ghosts of his family—in other words, a society of ghosts with periodic interludes of life on earth—made the step back into the ghostly family extremely easy, even, if you were sufficiently socially minded, distinctly desirable. And Buddhism, whose ideal required a man to renounce passion, possession, even affection, reduced all earthly interests to the lowest pitch, which was a continuous invitation to reduce them still lower, step off into death.

The early political character of the country bore in the same general direction. The clans abutted on one another. Frequent border disputes stimulated frequent resort to arms. The strength of the clan depended upon the loyalty of the retainer to the lord. There was need to fortify the walls of the castle, but there was even greater need to fortify the fighting qualities of the samurai who defended it. War was largely combat with swords. The individual's determination to fight to the end depended fundamentally on the psychology of loyalty. Whatever increased it would strengthen the clan. Obviously if you could make the retainer, because he felt he had been less loyal than he might have been, want to commit hara-kiri, you would to the uttermost have fortified the clan. Therefore, to make hara-kiri a shining act, however indirectly this was done, to dignify the act in every possible way, to surround it with ceremony, to train for it from youth, to have it done in the presence of others so that many eyes and many thoughts were turned on the one who was dying, to dramatize the capacity to suffer without giving any sign of pain, and to make the slightest disloyalty enough to bring it about, was of course to extract out of the practice the last drop of usefulness. A hara-kiri became a moral triumph.

That this explanation is likely is indicated further by the fact that hara-kiri was in high repute up to the time of the unification of the clans under the three strong Shoguns. Then it was forbidden. The united clans were now under one strong head, and the need to intensify clan loyalty was not only gone, but there was an advantage in weakening it. It would be wasteful to the united clans to have the best men kill themselves for a trifle. Hence the penalty for hara-kiri—the execution of the guilty one's entire family and the scattering of his house, the latter, of course, also giving unrest to the ghosts. It was to be expected that hara-kiri would come back into high repute as the hold of the Shoguns weakened and the clans began once more to compete with one another. So it did. And to lose repute again when the Imperial line returned to power over the renewedly unified nation. All through the Meiji Era a persistent effort was made to wipe out the practice. This was to be laid partly, too, to the passionate Westernization, even the feelings of the West imitated where they were not understood or felt—always to be remembered that the admitted purpose of this was to meet the West as effectively as possible when the West was to be met. Hara-kiri was then passed off smilingly as something belonging to a sentimental older day. But with the coming of the modern wars hara-kiri once more recovered repute, because now extreme loyalty to the nation was a value to the nation. We all know how the present Japanese army extols the supreme sacrifice.

There is a curious sidelight on Ito, revealing how far he was Westernized. This dates to his comparative maturity, because in his early youth he was, of course, as murderous and violent as anyone. Twice he repudiated hara-kiri. The first time, when it was a question of committing hara-kiri himself, he refused, took the Western point of view that it was cowardly, and said that he would fight his way out instead of cut himself open. The second time was when the guns were fired into Kobe with the foreign ministers in it. The man who had given the order confessed, undertook himself to assume the entire responsibility. Ito regarded it as "pitiful" that this man should commit hara-kiri, conferred with the British Minister to prevent it, and it was the Minister who insisted. That was a queer reversal: the Westerner, known traditionally to abhor such an act and in this instance privileged to prevent it if he chose, forced the Japanese to have it scrupulously carried out.

There are several sidelights from the life of Saigo. When Saigo was young a samurai saw him pound along the road, thought he would be a good one to repair a *geta*, which Saigo did. That was the lowest kind of work. The samurai now wanted a new pair made, and Saigo made them. The Rebellion came—and there was Saigo at the head of the troops, Commander. The samurai saw him, realized, wanted to commit hara-kiri. Saigo rebuked him vehemently—for daring to think of taking his life at a time like that. He could die—but in battle. In other words, there is a proper time for hara-kiri, and an improper. It will be remembered that Saigo let himself be exiled a number of times, did not complain, never mentioned hara-kiri, suffered boredom and torment—because that was what the Lord of Satsuma thought best. The big man became as meek as a girl. In other words, where suffering, enduring, forbearing, seem righter to the situation than suicide, the Japanese may take on positively early Christian states of mind, accept flagellation without protest. And, of course, Saigo died willingly enough when the right time came.

We Occidentals do not find it easy to die. We can get ourselves acquiescent and ready by thinking it over, but we do not take to it pleasantly. We are not fully sure of our immortality. Furthermore, we are less directly in touch with death. We have fewer deaths, as fewer births, are less violent by nature. Our social arrangements, our hospitals, even our undertakers hide death away from our sight, make it a fairly unfamiliar experience. Suicide with us represents usually a distraught mind, failure in life, need to escape from misery, an undoing of the normal personality, so that many psychiatrists believe suicide evidence of insanity. This may not always be true, but it certainly shows what we think of why the Westerner kills himself.

We would, I believe, need to go back here also to the mediaeval Europeans to begin to understand the modern Japanese.

So, hara-kiri is not really personal, or much less so than our suicide. The Japanese commits it by rule. The close of the war will tell us how often a Japanese officer has committed suicide rather than be taken prisoner. My guess is that it would actually occur often. The Japanese disposition to pattern response makes that likely. There is no bodily reason not to be taken prisoner by American or British troops, as most Japanese perfectly know, but in clan days it was easier not to be taken prisoner by your ferocious adversary, so that to kill yourself rather than surrender was raised to an ideal, and this pattern response became so strong that it determines action today when the facts no longer warrant it. That is part of the explanation. The other part is the advantage to any army—which the Japanese army always clearly saw—in having soldiers believe that it must be either victory or death.

Charles Boyer gave us a quite correct idea of hara-kiri on the screen. One felt sharply the source of the details of the ritual. The special genius of the Japanese is for life inside a room, a bare room whose whole adornment may be the individual who occupies it and the garments that he wears. Hara-kiri is no turning on of gas in a dark kitchen, or slumping over the steering gear in a night garage. The utmost is made of the central figure. The white cloth of

death is spread on the straw-matted floor. The hero settles
in the middle. His second helps him off with his outer
dark kimono, reveals him to have under it a white one,
the kimono of death. The second passes him an object
wrapped in white. The hero unwraps the object, a polished
dagger, the dagger of death. The second helps him to open
his kimono and bare his abdomen. He leans on the dagger
—like a surgeon, is careful to cut where there are few
blood vessels, the idea being he must not bleed too pro-
fusely and die too rapidly. His blood must not soil the
tatami. The dead body must show no sign of struggle, no
disorder in the posture. It is all somewhat the way a
Spaniard feels about a bull fight, not too much interest in
the fact of the bull dying, but very much interest in how
the bull dies—a little astonishing when the bull is yourself.
Everything about a hara-kiri is calculated for the maximum
effect upon the onlooker of this supreme spectacle. The
bare abdomen, the thrust, even the friend standing behind
and quickly finishing the job, all calculated to make a
scene. Where an enemy has appeared in the midst of the
deed, a victim has been known to clip off a piece of his
own gut and fling it with a gesture in the enemy's face.
Every Japanese schoolboy could relate to you the history,
the stories, and all the details of the orderly ceremony.
And many a father to this day trains his sons precisely
in the ritual.

The great hara-kiri of modern times was the well-known

one of General Nogi, worth repeating again because it
has been a powerful example, and will be the excitant to
the reckless deed of many an otherwise ordinary Japanese
soldier—in other words, will cost us lives. The General
was the commander at Port Arthur in the sanguinary
Russo-Japanese War. He was victorious, but the newspapers hinted that he had lost too many men, so he
offered to commit hara-kiri. The Emperor forbade him,
the old Emperor, grandfather of Hirohito. Nogi obeyed.
It is said that he made up his mind to the deed when he
overheard through a train window in a railroad station a
mother and a son, who did not know him, lay the death
of the boy's father to Nogi's strategy. It should be mentioned that General Nogi himself lost one son in the
attack of the famous 203 Metre Hill, another son at the
battle of Nanshan, and that he had only the two. But
now comes the queer primitive slant of the Nogi mind.
The war was in 1904-5. Six years elapsed. In 1911 Prince
Fushini set out on his celebrated tour of the world. Togo
was the principal attraction of that tour. Nogi was one
of the principal attractions. England and America wel-
comed the party with great enthusiasm. It was a long-
sustained triumph. That is, Nogi was traveling through
the West, immersed in Western feelings, Western scenes,
was no longer a figure merely of Japan but of the world.
Yet apparently only the surface was shaken, the depths
remained untouched. The next year, 1912, the Emperor

died. A week before the formal burial Nogi came to the
house of a friend, delivered him a poem, which seemed
to say that the master was dead and that now the servant
must go too. It feels for a moment like a situation in a
modern pathological drama. But it was not. It lay much
further back—the servant was following the master into
the world of ghosts to serve him there. Nogi may not have
explained it that way to himself, but it was plainly a
pattern situation out of the shadowy Japanese past. On
the day of the Emperor's burial, while all over Japan the
gongs were booming and the body was being carried up
the temple steps, the General cut open his abdomen,
followed his Emperor to the grave. And General Nogi's
wife followed him. They were going back to their ancestors,
and that primitive belief is still reality to them. The Nogi
shrine in Tokyo is one of the most visited in the Empire.
Nogi died September 13, 1912.

It ought to be added, though it is obvious, that hara-
kiri, like assassination, has for centuries been an acknowledged Japanese method of accomplishing political ends.
Hara-kiri and assassination are everywhere two sides of
the same grim coin.

CHAPTER THIRTY-FOUR
Sato's Daughter

I STAYED ON AT MAKURASAKI AND THEY TOOK ME TO house industry after house industry, one day to the silkman.

On shelves heaped with mulberry leaves were silk worms. Thousands and thousands of worms. Body on body. Clay-colored. And but for this color these thousands might have been thousands of infinitely tiny alligators. Especially the heads. But yet too active for alligators. Nibbling, nibbling, nibbling. One rose up, stood, balanced itself on almost the tip of its tapering end. Rose too far, swayed, bent, fell, its mouth square upon the edge of a tender mulberry leaf. The worm tasted the leaf. Moved its head to the left. Tasted again. Still further to the left. There it found what it sought, began at this point, ate for a quarter of an inch, then shuffled back, and continued so, each journey of the head deepening the scallop that it dug. Then it began a scallop within the scallop, and another within that. Scallop, scallop, scallop. Each bite was so dainty that it seemed more a dissolving than a cutting. Nothing, I am sure, eats at its overwhelming dinner with so polite a restraint, and yet by evening this shelf of worms would have consumed all the leaves of two big mulberry trees. And there were shelves and shelves, all consumed with this same geometric neatness. The worms advanced with the patience of fate. Indeed, the whole march of their lives was like fate. Five days they ate, ate all the time that they did not sleep. Then for a day they starved. But only that they might eat with greater energy for five days more. Then again they starved. And again they ate. Then, abruptly, they ate no more. They seemed to have eaten themselves into a stupor, or that is how they lay about. But it did not seem like stupor either. It seemed more like some state of dreams. The clay bodies had become like some ancient glass. A transparence was over them. Other things in nature have that transparence, too, when they are about to give birth. Within an hour the worms would have begun to work upon the cocoons. Four days they would work uninterruptedly. Then either they would break through their houses and go forth as butterflies, which was unlikely in the extreme, or Sato's daughter would drop them into boiling water.

Sato's daughter had not that kind of hardened look. She must not have thought of what she did. She kept her mind, no doubt, upon the silk. I saw her through a doorway across a yard where two uprighteous geese stood, like a design, in perfect parallel. Sato did not introduce me to his daughter—in the end she would grow up only to be a woman. She knelt there. Her kimono had slipped and bared her shoulder. A pale frail yellow land lily, I thought. One hand held the glass rod which kept the upper sheath of skeins separate from the lower. The skeins were yellow, came from cocoons that were a cross between the worms of Japan and the worms of Italy. Her face took some of the yellow, and her hair also, that even without this sheen would have been very light for a Japanese. Not once did she raise her eyes. Neither did her brother raise his. His were very black. Sato did introduce me to his son. The son was older than his sister. He was sixteen. But his sister would soon be a wife. The bridegroom was the son of the dyer. That last fact old Sato whispered to me. He and the dyer had had this union in mind for years. Both were from the same original family. That was good. And the match would be good, too, for both their businesses. As it was, their friendship alone had already made them the two strongest men in the town. Silk weaver and dyer! And the very best dyer in this part of the country!

Of course, between Sato's daughter and the son of the dyer there would be no need of a go-between. But Sato would have a go-between just the same. Otherwise a man could never be at his ease. There was Kamayama—that marriage was taken for granted practically from the time the two young ones were born. So old Kamayama thought he would settle it himself, not have a go-between, just

himself call on Miyahara and make the proposal for his
son. Old Kamayama was always a stubborn animal. What
was an ancient custom to him. He found out to his cost.
The match was off. And Miyahara was not a man to give
undue attention to form either. Nevertheless, the match
was off. Miyahara married his daughter to Iwaya's son
instead.

For an instant Sato turned again to silk, but the next
instant he said he was human. Silk did not interest him
really. A village like this was a natural place for gossip.
Gossip was its daily life. And about what could one gossip
so well as about an approaching marriage.

There was Nakamura. His case showed clearly how
times had changed. Everybody was laughing at Nakamura.
No one would have laughed at him in the old days.
Everyone would have regarded it as right, as it was, that
his brother should choose for him. His brother was the
oldest of the family, the sharpest, the richest, the best
able to make a match, and yet everybody laughed. The
Japanese world was ill. It was listening too much to the
West. It forgot to turn to itself, to the past, the ways
that had grown up in the East, that were part of the
blood and the being of the East. The family, the ancient
family, was losing its singleness. The clan was losing its
singleness. The nation would also. Too often of late the
old were not left the final word in a marriage. Imagine
that in his grandmother's day! Even in his mother's day!
There was a cousin of his mother's grandmother, married

against his mother's will—no one ever forgave her. Never. Dared marry outside the family! Marriages ought not to be outside the family. It would change the race. It would be worse even than the coming of Perry. It would be a break in the isolation where it could not be mended. Just anyone marrying anyone—bad. Imagine a mixed-up city like Yokohama producing a really good fighting man. No more important a question in Japan today than to whom shall one give one's daughter. Fools thought otherwise. Yes, the times were bad. Women even presumed to consider divorce. But not the dyer's son. And not his daughter. It was right that those two families should marry into each other.

And no doubt Sato knew of what he spoke. His daughter sat always in the same place, always the glass rod in her own hand, the skein moving forward, forward, forward. Yet as I looked into that intelligent quiet face, I wondered if after all it did not hold some other thought, some thought of its own. "Look at her," said Sato. "Have you any idea of what she is doing? Weaving the silk of her own wedding dress. This will be an ancient marriage. The bride will wear three dresses. The first will be full of color, and gay. The dyer will see to that. The second will be gay too, but not so gay. The third will be white, signifying that this union will last forever . . . . But what does that mean to anyone nowadays . . . ."

CHAPTER THIRTY-FIVE
The Makurasaki Geisha House

MY HOST—THE MAKURASAKI OPTHALMOLOGIST—
walked near me. "The dinner is at the house of the geisha!"
He whistled the words, opened wide his slits of eyes, as
suddenly closed them again, and said no more.

A geisha met us in the garden and escorted us to the
pavilion. Tonight was a doctor's party. Twenty kneeling
figures of men bent as we approached, and together, in
silence, we watched the twilight move out to sea, for the
geisha house stood high over the sea. "Not by hand—by
water." My host, who was still near me, anticipated the
question I felt. There was a rock in the middle of the bay.
It was like a finger, and it pointed upward to the sky. It was
blacker as the light went out of everything but the west.
One had indeed to be told that it was not put there by
hand, that it was shaped by the eddying of the sea—a
slender finger exactly in the middle of a circular bay.

When the lanterns were brought we found ourselves
outside a large oval of lacquered tables. This was not the

daily rice, fish, and tea. This was a banquet. Under cover of bowls were eggplant broiled in soya sauce, gingko seed pierced with pine needles, toasted eel, bamboo sprouts, plums pickled in perilla.

The women had worked noiselessly. They knelt in the central space, composed and smiling. I had asked the Grandmother at Funakura what happened to the geisha as her youth went by. She shook her head, and I could learn no more than, "Only if she has a beautiful heart or a beautiful face—else there is no escape." My host, who had once been in America, had a notion how the scene should daze me, impenetrable eyes watching while I in kimono ate raw fish by lantern light. I was surprised to hear him speak of it. The tone had been so natural that I took as natural, too, the extraordinary facts.

Opposite each gentleman sat his geisha. There were four opposite me. Our conversation went by smiles and bows and oglings till it occurred to one of them, came to her clearly as a small revelation, that she might make him who had been in America give her the use of speech. Henceforth there was a buzz borne continually between us, and each response was greeted by bubbles of laughter. All wanted to know the byways of the Western knowledge of heart.

Three of the four were fluffy and merry, and the wine glossed their faces. The life suited them. The fourth was slight and pale, drank much, yet was no part of the felicity,

looked as if cigarettes might hold the rein. She lit one,
puffed twice, handed it to me, then observed me with such
a skew intentness as I smoked that the three fluffy ones
glanced at each other and smiled. My bowl she filled with
shotsu, then with *sake*, then with *shotsu*, then with *sake*,
and each time I did not drink snatched up the bowl and
drained it to the lees. Presently she quit the room, returned
with a bottle of French wine. But when I still only sipped
she was confused and sidled over to the gentleman who
was supplying speech. He laughed at what she said, the
fluffy ones moved in close and laughed too, and when my
pale one came back to me she wanted to know, Did I
love her?

The pitch of the party rose by degrees, though the talk
remained low and the wooden crack of the breakers on
the beach was as loud as before. It was less and less like
the West. In his cups the Japanese may grow only the
more heavily moody. He has the appearance of hot speech,
but he does not speak. The women stayed within the
oval, the men without. The tête-à-tête was always across
the lacquered tables, more impassioned, more as if each
pair were alone, yet none touched, none kissed. The pale
one came with wine and more wine. Her eyes showed it,
not unbeautifully, but otherwise she knelt as she knelt,
gazed as she gazed. Her kimono was a rich purple with
white birds on the wing, and in a lantern light that
swooned with smoke she was such a disengagement of sex

from the burden of it that I admitted to a stunned happiness, and when she begged to be taken to America with the other of my women I was not altogether pleased that the times were out of joint.

Would she have gone? She was young. She was already worn out. Who knew enough about the foreigner to say it would not be easy for him to buy one from this life? She may have thought she detested Japan, and it would not be remarkable if she detested her portion of it. America or Timbuktu. One must have had some experience with Timbuktu to realize that no romance wide of one's self is likely to remain happy. I asked my host how old she was, and whether it was probable one so young would have gone far on the primrose way. He said it was not probable, and he asked her how old, and she told him she would soon be fifteen—fourteen, according to our calendar. By the time she was eighteen she would have had many many lovers. Later her head drooped, and she slept there as she knelt. She was more daintily artificial than ever. Once she roused, but only to rest the tip of her forehead against a beam.

CHAPTER THIRTY-SIX
Women

IN PRE-WAR JAPAN THERE WERE SALESLADIES, NURSES, schoolteachers, secretaries, hairdressers, woman doctors, woman scientists, even woman streetcar conductors, all the categories, many in the low categories, few in the high, the history of a woman in any one category differing from that of an American woman only as Japanese life differs from America life. The institutions of wife and geisha, however, are unique.

To begin with, the Japanese male does not think of sexual intercourse as we do. He thinks more biologically. I spoke once to the eminent Kitasato of the Institute of Infectious Diseases. He had a student who also had attained eminence, in bacteriology, and, as was well-known, had let that student slip through his fingers. I reminded him of this. He admitted it freely. He was hoarse as he spoke—had a malignancy of the throat of which he was to die—and the German came in blasts from his short powerful body. "I knew he had talent. But I would not allow anyone that irregular in my laboratory. I would not allow anyone to come and hang his hat, then go and carouse three weeks." I suggested that a Japanese student might live a more active sexual life than an American student was apt to have the opportunity or inclination to lead, and Kitasato absent-mindedly agreed, but then vigorously corrected: "As to that, that makes no difference. I was interested only in his irregular hours—not in what he did with them." Sex is satisfied like hunger. There is not around it that wide aura in which so much of the psychologic interest of Western life lies. And the psychologic life would be more divergent still if it were not true that we also, once the early blush of love is paled, fall back frequently on building a life out of a relation that has less to do with sex and more to do with practicality.

The life of the Japanese woman seems a colorless sequence. The girl-infant is received indifferently. The oldest girl-child takes care of the next oldest, and so on down—at least so it was in several houses. The young woman marries or enters a geisha house or goes to work. If she goes to work her life to our eyes is unmitigatedly dreary. If she enters a geisha house it is perhaps as Grandmother said, "Only if she has a beautiful heart or a beautiful face—else there is no escape." If she marries she gives up her own ancestors, her own house gods, her own cult, her own family. To be a daughter-in-law anywhere in Asia is not a happy state. She becomes a mother, has child on child. Should she live long enough, as an aging woman she attains at last to a position of personality and power. But that is not all of the story.

First, we must admit that there is this to be said for the Japanese relation of the sexes—a healthy family does result. A strong and, up to now, enduring nation does result. Howsoever undesirable the life of the Japanese woman, that life does give solidarity to the Japanese home, which would be a point of interest to any government, especially of interest to any army, and of some interest also to the persons concerned. There must be something satisfactory to the husband, satisfactory to the wife, and satisfactory to the geisha. It is worth considering separately each of these classes.

How, or to what degree, is the life satisfactory to the Japanese husband. He begins with no romantic background built up from his earliest youth, as we do, though we do less than we did. Meanwhile there is no taboo about sex. Presently his family arranges a marriage. He lives with his wife. He is taken care of physiologically. He starts his own family on a basis which, because it is fairly cold, is fairly apt not to disillusion him. If he feels the need to flirt he goes to a geisha house. He is not going to marry a geisha, or very rarely. And the fact that that possibility is not always half in his mind makes his relation to the geisha simpler, less restless than usual flirta-

tions, and satisfying in as far as it quiets the needs that
he was feeling for a few hours of romance. You have
read of geisha taking away husbands, but I suspect that
it is rather a sadness in the life of geisha that the chance
of this is so rare. The husband has his wife, his occasional
geisha, may have his concubine. And there has never been
much question but that the ordering of Japanese sex life
was satisfactory to the male.

How, next, or to what degree, is the life satisfactory
to the Japanese wife? She also has no romantic background
built up from her earliest youth. Life is grayer along the
whole course. She marries. She has had no flirtatious
relation with her man, usually. She never will have,
usually. There is comparatively little romance. She built
up no illusions beforehand, builds none now, so loses none.
That all makes for stability in the house, whatever else
may be said about it. I do not mean by that that the
relations of Japanese husbands and wives are charmless
or cold. Until late years when we began rightly to detest
the Japanese, it was the whim of a number of Western
writers to say that the Japanese women made the best
wives in the world. The way a Japanese put it to me was:
"Foreigners of all nationalities who marry Japanese
women are sure to be fully satisfied, regardless of whether
they be Formosan, Korean, Chinese, or Occidental."
However that, the charm, the play, the intimacy of husband and wife is not that based on something delightful

partly because unsatisfied, but on the warmth that comes out of full satisfaction unblurred by romantic disillusion. A child arrives. The mother nurses the child. It is much easier in Japan to get mother's milk than cow's milk though it has been increasingly easier to get cow's milk in the last two decades. Anyway, a second child arrives, and in the country districts the mother may still be nursing the first, so nurses both. Her husband may very well in this time have felt the centrifugal urges that took him to the geisha house or lower. He may have slept with the geisha, but his wife will not be jealous. At least she is less apt to be jealous than the woman of the West, partly because the whole training of herself and her race has been against jealousy, and partly because she knows that the chance is overwhelming that her husband will remain her husband, her house remain her house, and her family only grow in numbers. She is the mother of his children, and there are usually soon an insuring number of them. If you were to remove all related apprehensions from a Western woman's jealousy, I imagine you would reduce it considerably.

A Western woman may be only revolted at the idea of so many children, and at this whole simplification of the roles of man and woman—even at the fact of an unfaithful wife being fairly unheard of, because, as a Japanese explained to me, "there is no machinery for." And I am certainly not suggesting that our women might want to

change places with the Japanese. I am only over-simpli-
fying so that we may put ourselves at the back of the
Japanese woman's mind. Otherwise it becomes impossible
for us to see how she is able at all to bear her life, let alone
to comprehend the quiet happy lives that Japanese women
live, especially lived in the years before the country ran
to the pain and impoverishment of war. Her house by
Western standards was a place of much work, but work
that devolved fairly enough on everybody. And I think it
needs not much imagination to understand the last point
in the comparative acceptability of her life: namely, the
older she grows the bigger her family and the greater
her dominance. Which is not only a satisfaction to her
old age, but a satisfaction toward which she may look as
she moves toward old age. The reverse of that is sometimes
the spectre at the back of our own women's lives.

Our women make a family of one or two, have them
before they are thirty or thirty-five, and from then on
the woman is apt to seek, more or less nervously, and
more or less enrichingly, to lead the life of her husband.
The Japanese woman is close to the life of her husband,
is interested in his affairs, in his success or failure, is always
talking business with him, but there is absolutely no competition with his external life—not even social competition,
the competition of talk, of having or not having ideas, etc.
That last has its obvious horror. But the woman does still
occupy completely the simple biological place. And

that is, of course, a strong place, established slowly and over such millions of years that the new place of woman, in the Western sense, is perhaps still largely to be achieved. Hence often the new woman's unrest. The Japanese woman has not that particular unrest. I speak, of course, of the Japanese woman in the Japanese town, not the emerging one in the capital. I myself would not like to lead the Japanese woman's life if I were a woman, but I must admit that she is so manifestly woman that she causes one sometimes to think of our women and realize how unestablished their position still is. And it does not dispose of the facts and the questions to simply dismiss the Oriental woman with such expressions as "breeding mare" or "milk cow." For it certainly is conceivable—if ever for some reason the life of the Western woman grew hard enough, if she grew more and more nervous—that the need to be the more earthly woman could reassert itself irresistibly.

How, next, or to what degree, is life satisfactory to the Japanese geisha? The first point, that we all know, and that outrages us so as to make everything else difficult to examine at all, is that the girl sells herself or is sold into the geisha house. The system is slavery. But at least there is this one initial mitigation, that when the girl is sold she has never had the romantic hope that lies at the back of the minds of most girls in the West, or certainly far from as much of it. She is sold in every kind of way, more brutal, less brutal, with more of her consent, with less of her consent. The family property is mortgaged, and she sells herself to clear it. She thinks her brother ought to have the higher modern education, and she sells herself to get it for him. A man above her station loves her, is unhappy he cannot marry her—if she went into a geisha house he and she might have much of one another. But the life, too, may be the life of her talent. She will be trained—may begin as early as her fifth year—to sing, to dance, to wait on men, to talk to men, and to talk to them mostly when they are warmed with *sake*, to think of ways to excite their talk when they are disposed to be gloomy. She may be attached to one geisha house, subject to call at several, or for particular men, or for particular men parties. She may have a "patron." She may accompany men on an excursion into the country. I remember a party that came trout-fishing from Kagoshima to Maku-rasaki, twenty-five men and twenty-five geisha. The guide did the fishing, the geisha sang and fried fish, the twenty-five men ate. One grew tipsy. This is what he said. "Ah, but trout is real sport to fish! And there is always the geisha. There must be the geisha. Just as one kind of womanly nearness depresses life, so does the other enhance." An entirely unsentimental Japanese assured me that with a well-trained geisha there was never a dull moment. No matter how self-centered a man was, or how

timid, or how awkward, the geisha would make it possible
for him to be at ease and fairly happy.

The return of the geisha to the free world does not
depend on herself, and that is almost the greatest curse.
She must be bought. She cannot earn her way out. At
the best, a lover buys her, but though this is a common
theme in Japanese stories I am certain it is not common
in Japanese life.

What has she to look ahead to? In late years, because
of war and the preparation for war, her activity has been
much suppressed, but yet she has had the stimulation of
the more relaxed hours of men. Generally everything
depends on her talent, and on her beauty. Generally I
think it must always be a worried life. It has every quality
of courtesan feeling in it. Sad twisted moments. Hearn
tells of O-Kama of Osaka, who "collected from the funeral
pile the ashes of her lover, mingled them with *sake*, and
at a banquet drank them, in the presence of many guests."
Japanese men are apt to paint for you an idealized picture
of the geisha, and slur over the fact that they do not last
long—or, if they do last long, why are they all so young
except for the few older ones that you see serving as
matrons? Japanese wives, the few times I have had any
chance to get an opinion from them, seemed to me truly
indifferent to the geisha, and to their husband's relation
to the geisha, seemed to feel the geisha were creatures
caught. One of them said: "It amuses the men and keeps

them alive, in that way. Afterward they come home, to a haven, to rest." The geisha's life is usually a laborious life. As she grows older her hopes of being drawn out in marriage grow fainter. She will be less and less useful to the geisha house. She may become the cleaning woman. She may be allowed to leave, and work in a munitions factory. She may, and often does, go downhill to the Yoshiwara, or she may be lucky and instruct into her kind of life the coming generation. The old geisha in Maku-rasaki used to teach the children of the town how to dance and sing, used to go with them in a flat-bottomed boat, slowly 300 feet up the river, slowly 300 feet down the river, for hours, and you could hear her voice pierce over the town, a very high falsetto. Or she may be a matron in a geisha house. I remember particularly one such leading a blind singer, who would visit a while at each of the men's parties, to sing a lament of Saigo.

But, of course, in one respect all this is not too completely different from the hopes and hopelessnesses of some of our own women. After all, many a private secretary spends much of her day making dentist appointments for her employer's children, reminding him to remember his wife's birthday, or his own wedding anniversary. She gets her salary. She is not sold. That is the tremendous, the unbridgeable difference. But she is apt to dress to please her employer, worries about her figure because it lessens her chance of holding her job or getting

another. You need only to sit down at the table in a lunch-
room of schoolteachers, or at a business woman's club
when there are not too many around, to remember that in
all countries there is the pain of facing old age unprotected.
The geisha has that pain in an exaggerated way.

The geisha system supplements the Japanese family
system. The slight ceaseless flirtation that goes on day
and night in the West—in the restaurant, at a street
corner, in a movie, at a cocktail party—is more segregated
in Japan. At least, since a man's house is apt to be a
soberer place with emphasis on the children, the geisha
house gets to be a concentrated release of that so-called
masculine side of him. I remember a father of many
children, whom I had seen only in his own house, fall into
conversation with a geisha under the softening influence
of *sake*, and I could not believe it was the same man. He
had positively a kind of frivolity in him. And that is the
geisha house's function. And the system is of importance
in the war because it does represent a union of the males
of the nation by still another bond—especially in those
years of preparation that went before the war, during the
whipping up of the fanatic patriotism. The system, like
everything Japanese, is closely knit, closely controlled.
There are high geisha houses, there are low geisha houses,
but they are all essentially the same, not like anything
else on earth, not like the Chinese sing-song house either,
and they cement into one the whole male recreation life

of the nation. They are the place of hot talk stimulated
by flirtation, consequently of the preparation for hot
deeds. They may make the male more male, may make
him coarser, more vigorous, freer of his home, more
swashbuckling, and they certainly make the Japanese mind
more devious for us to understand.

Business men transact business in a geisha house. In
a town like Makurasaki you may meet there the oph-
thalmologist, the mayor, the Buddhist priest. The Japanese takes his foreign guest to a geisha house. If he takes
him instead to his home, the guest will probably not see
his wife. She may come a moment to the polished veranda
outside the room and bow several times, and the guest
and the husband not necessarily pay any attention to her.
She hardly will eat with the guest. The wife of the
surgeon in Kagoshima was almost mysteriously out of the
room as soon as her husband entered. One always realized
sharply at such a moment that the family life of a man
is one thing, his social life another. There are no man-
woman parties in Japan. There could be no father's night
at a P. T. A. A man may also spend the evening in a
geisha house by himself, squat in a small partitioned room,
think and smoke, the geisha come and go or squat across
from him and gossip interminably.

An interesting sidelight on the relation of geisha and
wife to the man is given in Tsurumi's novel, "The
Mother." That relation was so understood by both that

when the man died, his wife, who was indeed a generous
and understanding person, visited the geisha, and they
exchanged sympathy, the one who had lost her best friend,
whom she had loved, and the other who had lost her
husband, whom she had loved. The geisha apologized to
the wife but admitted that she had burned incense to his
ghost. The wife invited her to continue to do so. They
parted with warmth and respect on both sides. It is true
that when the wife first found out that her husband was
visiting one particular geisha, it gave her pain.

We must be careful not to trust too far the Japanese
novel. With everything else before the beginning of the
century the novel was undergoing change. It forsook
imagination. It went out with open arms to realism. It
turned to the psychological, and, as has happened elsewhere, mainly to the ugly in the psychological. To read
it gives one a much more emphasized sense of a dis-
integrating society than the facts of Japanese society
perhaps warrant. The simple, smiling, open-hearted
woman that Lafcadio Hearn and Basil Chamberlain saw
and described, is undoubtedly much of the strength of the
present nation. The new woman may give some direction
to the keel of the nation but the strength that drives it
forward, on this side also, is the simpler, older, opener,
less psychologic being that we know was there, is there,
and can, of course, be no more wiped away than her
corresponding Western sister. As long as this woman

stands on her own she will continue to add power to the nation, but when, as is inevitable, she begins to change in the direction of the West, she will enter into a transitional stage of unrest, and to some degree unsettle the nation.

In Japan they are always careful to tell you that the geisha system is not harlotry, and this is true, though it does inevitably reach down to that indefinite line where harlotry begins. I saw a chalk-water sign written on the wall of the employment bureau at Makurasaki. It read:—

Wanted

One first-class geisha
Three second-class geisha
Two prostitutes
Three maid-servants

Add to that list, *One wife,* and you have pretty well covered the Japanese feminine range.

CHAPTER THIRTY-SEVEN
She Was Once a Geisha

I STOPPED FOR A NIGHT IN A HOTEL. A RUN-DOWN PLACE in a run-down town. Four rooms on a second floor, portable paper panels between them, more or less shut. Rain beat on the tile roof and was blown in noisy gusts against the night boarding. I lay in the wet thick air. If I turned my head I could see into the next room. In there was an old man with a cough. After a time the servant slipped into his room, arranged the bedding, wanted to slip out, said she had much to do, but he stopped her. They began to talk. He wanted her to help him to sleep. Sleep had been more and more difficult in the late years, and he was not used to travel, had not traveled since the Russian War. But now he was going far. He was going to visit the Great Shrine. He had saved for this journey for about fifteen years. He had saved twenty *yen*, and now he was going to spend the twenty all at one time. The servant must see to it that he got the lowest possible rate. He had not enough money to waste any on a room. And he had been walking already the last three days. She must not let him oversleep. He must be awake at 4 a. m. He would wake of his own accord, no doubt, and perhaps would not sleep at all, but if he should by some mischance happen nevertheless to fall asleep she must not let him spoil what it had taken him so many years to bring about.

To all this she nodded her head. To each of his many repetitions she gave her assent—repeated the same words quietly, calmly, reassuringly, treated him like a father. She was very young.

He went on—told her of next year and the years to come—how he would relate in his village his experiences, how much there would be to relate, all about the saving too, how he and his wife had talked and talked of this journey. His wife was dead now. Even if she had lived there would not have been money enough for two. But his wife would have understood that, of course. She would have wanted him to go alone.

The servant had put up the mosquito-net tent, knelt outside, a black shadow. Sometimes she shook her head. Often she said: "Hi, hi." He talked on and on and on, in a low mumble. She listened. She laughed from time to time artificially. Several times she struck her knees with her hands. Then she said she had been a geisha once—in the capital—in Tokyo!

At last the old man fell asleep. Quietly the shadow reached under the mosquito net, moved the tray with the tea and the tobacco *bon* away from his head, pushed over a panel to give him more air, silently slid away. She had stayed there with that old man the greater part of the night. She would not even ever be such an old man's dead wife.

CHAPTER THIRTY-EIGHT
Aritomo Yamagata, Soldier

IF THERE IS ONE JAPANESE MORE RESPONSIBLE THAN any other for the present Pacific war, the man is Yamagata, dead twenty-one years. In peace he planned war. In war he planned future war. I think it might be useful to look also at a portrait of him. The world knew him little.

Yamagata built the Japanese army. He wedged that machine so rigidly into Japanese civil life that any hand which has tried to tear out that dead man's work has always seemed weak, whereas the hands that furthered it have seemed stronger than they were.

Yamagata arranged it that the Ministers of Navy and Army in the Japanese cabinet must always be high ranking officers, then himself appointed every high ranking officer of his time, and thus controlled the cabinets. When he died his rule lived after him. If today a cabinet does not please Navy or Army no high ranking officer will enter it, and the cabinet cannot form. That is perhaps the fundamental plank in Japanese military might.

What you feel in Japan is that Yamagata's memory is held in an immense but chilled respect. He is no hero. There must be conflict in a hero's life, some kind of successful or unsuccessful opposition to what is around him, and in Yamagata's life there never was. He went against no current, went rather with a fundamental instinct of the nation, therefore never stood alone, had no failure, no sadness. He was simply one of a long line of war lords, the embodiment in his time of the soul of his people, that is profoundly warlike. An elderly organizing genius. His plans had the look of lasting till doomsday. His face had that look too. The skin lay economically close to the bone. A face dedicated to duty. But highly intelligent. In the older photographs also the signs of the physical suffering of a stubborn man who had fought long with an enemy inside him, dyspepsia.

He was born in the south, Ito's clan, Choshu, in the year 1838. A poor family with nothing to lose—usually said to be a good way to start life. The father composed poems. The son composed them also—but later when there was time for that. As young as they would let him he enlisted in the service of the clan as a common soldier. For a while he attended the same hero school as Ito—squatted not inside the room but beyond on the polished veranda, because he was less well-to-do. Possibly already there made mental notes on Ito, whom he was to understand icily well.

By the time of the war of the Restoration he had had

enough military experience to be Choshu's outstanding military man—not as outstanding as Satsuma's Saigo, but he was eleven years younger. He was never to have the color of Saigo. Did not want it. Power, not color. For pre-Restoration days he felt nothing but contempt. "Peace universally reigned. The swords were kept in their sheaths, and the arrows lay untouched in their quivers. Luxury and effeminacy followed in the wake of these." And of the war of the Restoration he said: "Not only did it save our country from the misfortune that befell our neighbor, China, but opened the pathway of civilization to our land." At the beginning of the war Yamagata was twenty-nine. Saigo was commander of the forces of the Emperor and he put Yamagata in charge in the field—saw in him the capacity for detail, the fatal steadiness, did not love him, yet gave the authority to him. The Restoration achieved, Yamagata was made Under-Secretary of War. The Under-Secretary set to work, silent sedulous work, utterly congenial to him, building the army. He was sent to Europe to see how things went there—henceforth Japanese were to fight not against Japanese, but against the West. It was in the year of the Franco-Prussian War, and he served with the French troops as observer at some of the most important engagements. The new Japanese army up to now had been modeled after the French. The French were beaten. The Japanese army was hereafter in many departments modeled after the German. But his most crucial observation was that in political Germany the army was free of the civil authorities. In later years he was to pursue this end relentlessly for his own army, with consequences for the world.

He returned from France in 1871. In 1872 he introduced universal conscription. He abolished the samurai, made the wearing of the two swords a criminal offense. This was drastic. In a place like Kagoshima the tone is such that even today you can still practically see the samurai striding over the roads and streets. Kagoshima was outraged. But there was a compensation. Henceforth soldiering was for everybody—everybody could be a samurai, as everybody had always wanted to be. The individualism would be gone and a fateful organization take its place. However, the national army was not truly national for some time yet. The Grandmother at Funakura told ruefully how there was continuous manipulation to make officers come out of the old samurai class, and privates out of the commoner class. The actual drilling of the new army first was entrusted to foreigners. French instructors, then some German and a few Italian, and gradually Japanese were substituted. Yamagata meanwhile had risen to Commander-in-Chief. Kirino, who was to fight with Saigo in the Rebellion, and Tani, who was to fight against Saigo, both had high commands.

Saigo himself had soon resigned—the general efficiency too much for his stomach. He was warmer, humaner, larger mold, more romantic. In 1877 came the Rebellion. The new army was set against the samurai army, and the samurai army was crushed. This was the test and the proof.

Yamagata went unswervingly on with the plan. All able-bodied Japanese males on reaching twenty were subject to service. This service was for three years, whereupon they were placed in the first reserve for two years, then in the second reserve where they were subject to call only in case of national emergency. The length of service of the first reserve was later greatly increased. All exempted for any reason were to constitute the militia. Non-commissioned officers were selected by the officers of the troops and altogether on the basis of merit. Commissions were granted only for actual service and at the end of rigid competitive examinations. Since the initial selection depended entirely on the physical state of the creature, and since the creature was instinctively military, there was a craving to get into the service, those selected regarding themselves as fortunate, those dropped into the militia as disgraced. Here lay one strength of the army. The individual soldier had zeal. He had a sense of opportunity. The world outside could know nothing of this. The numerical strength had comparatively little to do with the real strength, and the published figures could never be trusted, the Japanese being in a better position to keep secret their figures, also to conceal the possibilities of mobilization, as also the actual beginning of mobilization. We have never been able to keep a tab on Japan as we have on all European countries.

Conscription began in 1872. By 1888 it was admitted by the Japanese that it would be possible on three days' notice to place in the field 150,000 well-trained men with 120 guns, and 500 cavalry. The man power was taken with the mud of the farms still on it, and was therefore at once in good marching state. It needed no hardening. Nothing could be harder than the life it had come from, in spite of which fact even the Japanese have always said that the service was rough. It had the usual advantages for the physical nation, was exercise with a moral purpose, bleak survival-of-the-fit preparation of the body for the state, and were it not for the inevitably cruel use to which it must be put, would represent a period that might not be bad at the back of any man's life. Older Japanese officers look like prize fighters at the weighing-in—against the officers of most of the West, who look like university men. Apparently from the very start there was a carelessness about dress—spotted boots, untrimmed uniforms, unshaven faces. There is so much psychology in everything Japanese that one wonders whether the unkempt state was not deliberate, to keep the soldier further from the West, nearer to himself, nearer to that warring savagery that was his long heritage, and at the same time keep away suggestions of inferiority to the West. Add to the rough peasant faces, the squat bodies, the short legs, the animal alertness, the animal habits, and you understand why Japanese troops are apt suddenly to make you think of chimpanzees. We might in this connection remember that you control chimpanzees, as any scientist who has worked with them will tell you, not by denying them their qualities, but by admitting these, whereupon sometimes a frail scientist, because he knows just what the reactions of his animal-subject are, is able to manage it neatly.

During the building of this new army the Emperor Meiji stepped in wherever necessary to support it. He was friends with Ito and he supported Yamagata. He had no ambition to be the manifest Emperor, except as that might at moments be useful to the nation. He was able always to think only of the nation. Therefore he could come in powerfully to squash opposition when opposition became destructive. And, of course, he thought that the nation owed everything to the army. There was a question of a large army budget. It caused a storm in the Diet. The Emperor stepped in. "At this period if time is squandered in dispute and ultimately the great objects in view become neglected, so that the opportunity of promoting the nation's welfare and extending its influence are lost, the desire we cherish in view of meeting the spirits of our ancestors will be frustrated, and the way to reap the fair result of constitutional government will be missed . . . . As to the military defenses of the state, a single day's neglect may result in a hundred years' regret. We shall Ourselves economize in the expenditures of our household . . . ."

The Sino-Japanese War began in July, 1894. The quick succession of victories seems to have taken even Japan by surprise. If Yamagata was surprised no one will ever know. As a matter of fact, once the war was started, the fate of China was sealed. Japan was detailedly ready. China would have had to get ready in the course of the war, which was impossible. Characteristic Japanese capacities and characteristic European capacities functioned together in the new army. Throughout the campaign hand-carts carrying 350 pounds were drawn each by three coolies. At the same time a telegraph system, tried out in the Rebellion, was employed with great perfection, lines being quickly run right up to the edges of Port Arthur, so that the Imperial staff, which had promptly moved from Tokyo to the west coast, was in instant communication with the shifting troops. In this highly socialized army an unusual freedom of action was nevertheless allowed to all individual military units—to whole armies, to divisions, to individual men. A task once assigned was independently carried through. I have listened to a Japanese doctor describe how, despite the cost of continuous renewal, vaccines and sera were always ready for inoculation of two hundred thousand men on twenty-four hours notice. European science and Japanese efficiency.

Yamagata was ill from the start of the war, commanded from his army cot, grew more and more ill, was advised by his physician to return to Japan, refused, had finally to be ordered back by the Emperor. Marshal Oyama remained in the field to perform brilliantly, but the Yamagata war plan would in any case have unfolded in its own fatal way. Yamagata had henceforth the gray power of a chief-of-staff far from the battlefront, who nevertheless determined every move of the battle. He continued ill to the end of the war. He was chronically ill afterward. He was never again to accompany the army. He was to work diligently inside the Tokyo war offices. He preferred that. He was to bind his nation hand and mind—or, as he would have thought but not said, have it prepared for its destiny. He would be honest to the army. He would be utterly unscrupulous to the civil state, would employ chicanery, bribery, misuse of friendship, packed parliamentary session, even assassination—and he would be careful to do none of this so that it could be documentarily proven.

The Sino-Japanese War out of the way, he did not lean back on his accomplishments but began methodically to prepare for the next war. He did not slightly increase the army, he doubled it—this immediately on the heels of a successful war. He wrung unprecedented budgets from the unwilling parliament. The country rocked in a new financial scandal every month, but the number of *yen* that the army was allotted to spend was the exact number it spent. Yamagata kept his eye personally on every *yen*, and on every gun. Because the parliamentary life was so full of discord, immaturity, rottenness, a dust cloud lay also over the army's actual efficiency. No harm in that! How should the outer world suspect that in all this squabble there was a clear and cold and unrelenting mind. Yamagata took it for granted also that that next war would be a Russo-Japanese war. He made his arrangements. He did not need to tell his nation. He was one of those Japanese who never talk, or if they talk they say nothing, or if they say anything it is the reverse of what they mean. He could count on his nation because he was a genuine piece of it. He was in touch with its depths. When Ito went to Russia to see if he could negotiate a treaty, Yamagata let him—if a treaty should result, treaties had been broken before. The unyielding fact was—there would be a Russo-Japanese War.

The war began in February, 1904. It began in treachery. It ran its historic course. It culminated in victory. It almost established the Korean steppingstone onto the Asiatic mainland. Here are some sentences from Yamagata's own statement. "We came to the decision to forestall Russia in Korea, as the historical and geographical relations of Korea with our Empire demanded that we should have the peninsula in our power rather than it should fall into that of Russia. To attain this object we decided to construct the Seoul-Fusan Railway . . . . The naval forces of the two countries were almost equally balanced, but fortunately our navy had had experience in fighting in the past ten years, while Russia had had none . . . . We had no advantage over the Russian army, with the exception, as we thought, of the skill of our troops in fighting in such hilly country as Korea and Manchuria . . . . It was a critical and anxious time when hostilities were commenced, but the army was determined, we knew, to fight to a man in defense of the Empire. On the campaign being opened, however, we were able to attain a success far beyond that which we had hoped for. This was to be ascribed to the virtue of the Emperor and to the valor of the officers and men . . . . In deciding to conclude peace the government carefully investigated the present financial capacity of the Empire—the plans made for its future development—the general political situation of the world—as well as the fact that Russia was constantly aggressive and warlike . . . . The continuation of the war, it was thought, would only result to exhaust the funds required for the promotion of works in Korea and Manchuria. Thereupon the members of the government agreed without a dissenting voice to conclude peace without delay . . . . If the peace be condemned by some people, I for my part am quite willing to accept the name of being a member of the 'weak party'. . . . The government prosecuted the war with the greatest determination, and

is still competent to carry on. I have been in military
service over forty years, and through several wars. We
have experienced greater difficulty in other wars than the
one with Russia, though the wars of the past were of less
magnitude. We have always managed to overcome difficulties."

While the war was on there were no debates with Ito.
These were taken up again as soon as the war was over.
Japanese do not debate during war. In the debates Yamagata always won. His line was straight. First, he had
believed in the Restoration—which meant a strong clan
army. Then, he had believed in the test of the Rebellion—
which meant a strong commoner army. Then, direct action
in China—a strong national army. Then, direct action
against Russia—a strong modern army. Then, Korea
must be annexed. Ito stood in the way. Yamagata was
bland, dismissed the situation in Korea as unimportant,
actually said that it could safely be left for settlement
to the army! The debates between Yamagata and Ito
there at the beginning of the century paralled the late ones
between Japan and an outside world that was hopelessly
searching to find somewhere willingness to compromise.
Ito grew more and more insistent. Ito was really getting
to be troublesome. Up to now he had been a help—not
meaning to be, of course—because he kept off the other
nations. He kept other nations believing that Japan was
gradually moving toward modern conceptions of state.

Behind that protecting wall Yamagata had methodically and industriously worked. But now Ito was making this impossible. Accordingly Yamagata had Ito sent to Korea as Resident General. He was assassinated. Korea was annexed. And everything henceforth was easy. The government was a bureaucracy—and Yamagata appointed the bureaucrats. His hand on Imperial power was both direct and indirect. He was the intimate personal counsellor of the Emperor, and he was the leader of both the Elder Statesmen and the Privy Council. When the Emperor died, he was succeeded by a sickly son, so that the power more than ever lay in the now slowly aging, iron hands of the military master.

What he saw as Japan's next step we do not know—would hardly have known until he took the step. But that there was a next step we may regard as certain, because the building of the army went right on. When the Great War broke out Japan promptly added everything German in the Far East. That was easy, just a drill for the recruits and reserves who had not seen action in the Russian War. The cost was negligible. The gain looked small but was great. The army was stronger than ever, absolutely and relatively, for the armies elsewhere in the world were being decimated. Yamagata could quietly review his work and await events. Possibly the white race would destroy itself, as year after year it seemed bent on doing, in which case the problem of Asia would be simple indeed. Japan was at the high point of power.

Yamagata's workday was arranged on a rigorous schedule. It began always at the same hour. He had no confidants. If ever he allowed an interview the reporter went away with words, not news, flattered that he got into the house at all, and aware that he had been in the presence of a mountain of caution. For women the aging soldier could still unbend. He wore his medallioned uniform close around his gaunt body. He danced the classic dances with a grace. He made collections of samurai swords. He was married. Kokumo was his wife's name. Her family originally had thought him not good enough. There were no children. The marriage was satisfactory by Japanese standards. It went along year after year. Meanwhile he wanted his geisha pretty. Then he took an interest in one geisha. Sadako was her name. He set her up in his own house—with his wife—preferred to enjoy his concubine at home. That was a complicated strategic situation, not as extraordinary in Japan as it would be here, and not as extraordinary in that day as it would be today, but psychologically difficult anywhere and at any time, even in the Old Testament. But he managed it. After a time Kokumo died. He married Sadako. Another complicated situation, for Japanese society—its chief aristocrat marrying a geisha. But not a complicated situation for the aristocrat. He did in this world as he pleased. He won, won, won.

No international worries more than rippled the quiet. The world continued to know him little. Togo was known everywhere. Togo was the nation's display hero. Togo lived modestly in Tokyo, venerated, beloved, and without power. Yamagata had the power. He lived on and on, died February 1, 1922, at eighty-four, is still at this moment the most important man in Japan, because he built the army and choked constitutional government in the womb.

CHAPTER THIRTY-NINE
The Problem of the Language

Domei, the Japanese news agency, recently reported a meeting of scholars to choose 600 common ideographs that were to be issued in a pamphlet and distributed everywhere over east Asia to help the conquered peoples to an understanding of Japanese language, aims, culture, etc. The language barrier was admitted to be formidable. The pamphlet was to be called *Nihongo Hayawakari*, meaning Japan-language-quick-understanding. That sounds upstart, unimaginative, so dangerously lacking in humor that one is frightened vaguely that it could succeed, and the whole idea is thoroughly Japanese. But the Japanese language is undoubtedly difficult. Much in the past can be explained by that difficulty. It will be there in the future too. It is a problem of the war and of the peace. I do not have any idea how the problem can be solved.

It is necessary for the student of the written language to memorize two syllabaries. The syllabaries might be thought of as alphabets, except that the characters represent not single letters as in our language, but syllables. There are 51 symbols in each syllabary. And, besides these, the student must learn a huge number of Chinese characters. The Chinese characters were brought from Korea and China, and, depending upon the part they came from, the meanings vary. Thus there are apt to be four or five possible meanings for one character. And all these various methods of expression are to be found on the same page. You read them together. Two results are to be anticipated. One, until you have gone far in learning such a language you are too bewildered to understand anything. Two, after you have learned it, it is apt to have a great nuance and subtlety of expression.

About 1000 of the Chinese characters are said to be acquired in the elementary school. Between 2000 and 3000 are necessary for the reading of the daily newspaper. A well-educated person knows at least 5000. And several times that number exist. The difficulty of learning the language becomes, I think, plainer. The literacy of the country is always given as very high, 99.5%, often said to be the highest in the world, but that figure needs to be interpreted. Because obviously the Japanese must know his language very well indeed before it can be anything like as useful to him as ours is to us. In one analysis of the highest elementary class, out of 1356 possible characters, one pupil knew 1325, the average known was 600, and one pupil knew 27.

Foreigners, and also many Japanese, have been anxious to change the language. For a time there was a widespread effort to adopt the Western type of alphabet. This dropped off with the late surging fanatic conservatism and the general return to the old. All nations, of course, in times of intense national feeling are apt to go somewhat that direction, steer their populations onto their native languages exclusively.

I suspect that foreigners do not often get far in the mastery of Japanese language. Certainly, Japanese nationals were constantly in use as interpreters and translators by the foreign services. Basil Hall Chamberlain, who was in Japan long, early, and knew it well, confessed abjectly to the difficulties of the language. There is also a politeness factor that adds to the difficulty. A Japanese explaining it to me, said: "There are twenty ways of saying Mr., but every Japanese understands why each particular one is used, what degree of respect or disrespect it implies." That undoubtedly would be difficult for a foreigner. Lafcadio Hearn lived in Japan for fourteen years, had his limitations, was sometimes the most profoundly mistaken of the observers of Japan, but was generally the most accurate, had a sensitive instinct for the country, gave himself to it as no one else ever did, and was besides, a gifted linguist and literary man. Yet he also had difficulty with the language. He never used it freely. He never pretended to. The Japanese often ridiculed his speech. He was mostly not understood. This went deeper than speech and has a sad side. Hearn married a Japanese woman. "Even my own little wife is somewhat mysterious still to me though always in a lovable way. Of course a man and woman know each other's hearts, but outside of personal knowledge, there are race-tendencies difficult to understand." Mrs. Hearn wrote her reflections after his death. She had lived with him in greatest intimacy for fourteen years. She bore him three children. She had an active hand in his literary work, told him the stories that he retold, and contributed many strokes of color. And she does reveal some understanding of his art. But beyond that her understanding of him is achingly limited. Yet she had him alone—because he was singularly alone. In fact, her recollections make him more dreadfully alone than anything written of him, or than she had any idea. The volume by his son years later fills in more fully the days and nights, but the son had an artificially long chance to think things over, and the loneliness of Hearn's closing years is not essentially lifted. All of this should remind us of the confidence with which we sometimes announce our understanding of the Japanese, and they of us.

But, to return specifically to the problem of the language. The Japanese do not have the same difficulty in mastering English that we have in mastering Japanese. English is so very much simpler. It always surprised me to see Japanese in Tokyo riding in the streetcars reading *The Saturday Evening Post*. The Japanese who year after year passed through our country, often used our language with very considerable skill. I knew a Tokyo physician who knew it masterfully. There were occasional Japanese who did well with it even before the beginning of the century. Ito spoke an excellent, if slow and careful, English. Viscount Hayashi, Ito's contemporary, wrote a capable novel, as have a number of novelists since. *For His People* is the Hayashi novel. It ends with the execution of four small children in the sight of their parents. The mother, seeing the children one after another beheaded, goes mad, and curses the perpetrators, and the father takes up her curse and turns it into a prophecy of doom, the prophecy coming true, not supernaturally, but because the terribleness of the pronouncement works suggestively upon the minds of the doomed. It is a moving story. Hayashi wrote it in English. And his reason for writing it is worth noting: he wished to tell the outer world that the Japanese does not forget slights and wrongs. That is, this language-talented diplomat wrote a three-hundred-page threat. However, if thought of from the point of view of its success in expressing feelings, it is a very skillful if old-fashioned literary piece.

One might at the same time easily exaggerate how well the Japanese do know English. And only a very small part of the population does—for instance, not the police. The Japanese seldom learn to speak English with the ease that the Chinese on the same level learn, never with that indifference, possibly because the Japanese try too hard. I knew a man, very intelligent, who had studied English all his life, and for forty years had been surrounded by English-speaking students, and they constantly had trouble in understanding what he said. His own explanation was that his people were trained not to speak, were praised for silence and for brevity, and that, whatever else that might be worth, it did not develop the race's speech capacity.

Admiral Togo's case is interesting. In his boyhood he could of course not study English. English was forbidden along with all other intercourse with the foreigner. But with the Restoration and the decision to Westernize the country as rapidly as possible, and to arm it, the language of the barbarian became an obviously useful tool. Togo studied English in Tokyo when he was twenty-two and was just beginning work at the newly established naval academy. Soon he realized that the chance of learning it was practically better down at Yokohama, so he went there. Later he went to England, stayed for years, served on an English merchantman that functioned as a naval school, was addressed by English professors, for a time lived in an English household. Nevertheless when he returned to England on the triumphant world tour in 1911 he talked through an interpreter—preferred to. A Japanese would be inclined to lay this wholly to Togo's good taste, that did not let him speak the foreigner's language awkwardly.

My total impression is that an occasional Japanese may be said to speak a foreign language clearly, a good many speak it correctly, a rare one speaks it idiomatically, but I have no idea what people mean when they refer to many Japanese speaking it fluently. I always think that such people must have visited a very special Japan.

And it is what one would expect. Behind the symbols of a language there is a language brain, and the Japanese language brain has long been adjusted to such a complex process of expression that I would think it must inevitably have trouble with languages that are so very much easier. I do not believe this to be mere theory. There is an undoubted deviousness about the Japanese mind. Possibly the language is complicated for that reason. Or more likely the language—which came to the country in as fragmentary a way as its character suggests—has complicated the Japanese mind. I believe, indeed, that this is psychologically probable.

The Japanese interest in play on words is well-known. They prefer a word to have many meanings—this beyond the several meanings of each Chinese character, and the several meanings of the syllables in the two syllabaries. The fact may be a torment to anyone who gets to know a few Japanese persons fairly well. They prefer their meanings not to be entirely clear. Their poetry is, besides its often genuinely poetic content, very much an interest in the double and triple significance of words. I believe that a part of the pleasure they take in poetry is in the exercise of this species of ingenuity—ingenuity in creating their own poetic obscurities, and ingenuity in solving the obscurities of some other poet. They tell you that a hundred persons may interpret the same *hokku* in a hundred different ways, and that the interest in a *hokku* is heightened when it has that possibility. Almost every Japanese does sooner or later compose poetry. To his host. To his guest. Before his suicide. At a birth. At a death. At the coronation of the Emperor. At the performance of a play. It is said that a Tokyo newspaper offered a prize for a poem on the close of *The Doll's House*—on whether or not the play should have had its own ending or another—and the newspaper received 100,000 poems. Or, the Japanese composes poetry for no reason at all except that the evening is mild and the fireflies are prevalent. Japanese men have no feeling that the composition of poetry is feminine. And this widespread preoccupation with poetry, incidentally, keeps a lyricism over all levels of the nation, which it is quite easy for even a foreigner to perceive, a veneer of feeling, so that acts are not entered into coldly but with

that push that comes of slightly drunken emotions. Poetry
may cover the raw daily life, and also over such a thing
as war may draw a sheet that conceals the bloody mangled
soldier, leaves the heroic lines of a consecrated youth that
you would not even need to think had any touch of death
about it.

I believe it reasonable to assume that a language like
the Japanese, besides complicating the brain, and develop-
ing in it a capacity for the subtlety of meanings, might
run it toward deliberate verbal deception, occasional genius
for it, even produce in it some kind of shift so that truth
and lie got easily mixed. I need hardly add that such a
creative duplicity, innocent in the matter of language,
might appear in a less innocent form in a nation's capacity
for politics and diplomacy. That is, I do not think it is
fantastic to reason that to some degree Japanese language
has become a training school for the Japanese conception
of international honesty.

I like, however, to say frankly that I have no sympathy
with the disposition to make contemptuous humor of the
blundering speech of the Japanese hotel clerk, customs
officer, taxi driver, manservant of the foreigner living in
Tokyo. I have no sympathy with the implicit assumption
that literacy means to speak English. For the peace of the
world I would prefer that all nations spoke one language,
and I would not care too much what that language was,
though for the richness of the world I would prefer that

such a revolution did not come too soon. In a liberal era I suppose it is conceivable that we might induce the Japanese gradually to discard their language, since they went somewhat in that direction once. I like, furthermore, to say that I regard it as commendable in the Japanese, and unfortunate for us, that all our intercourse with him has been conducted in our language—English or some European language. It has inevitably given him, at least on one side, an understanding of us that we have not had of him. I would not know how to remedy that, but I would regard it as one of the facts to face. And also, since our intercourse with him has been conducted in our language, he has looked more awkward and immature than he is, has seemed less, and that again has been an advantage to him. By a similar reasoning, in any propaganda to Japan we should use not Japanese but English. English will reach few, but it will reach the important few, and our Japanese, if it actually gets all the way into the ear of anyone, will sound absurd, implicitly insult and therefore weaken us.

Language perhaps partly explains also the annoying character of the Japanese small official and the cruelty of the police. Only a fraction of the cruelty, to be sure, because the cruelty is partly the mediaeval mind and partly recent events—a suddenly swollen ego is apt to be cruel. But language incapacity may well be some fraction of the explanation of the clumsy, all-present, pin-pricking, gruelling, spying Japanese police. The policeman in Japan is

a small-salaried and at the same time important dignitary.
This is no recent innovation. He for many years has been
just that. I remember well the Funakura and the Makurasaki policemen—both of them men of good families that
came down in the world. The difference in late years is
the enormous increase in the number of such small-salaried
important dignitaries. That class of man everywhere, but
perhaps especially in Japan, is natively suspicious, a sus-
picion that would hardly be reduced by two decades of
running down of "dangerous thoughts." Toward the foreigner the police's relation has been especially wrong.
Everyone knows of the police's difficulty in understanding
the language of the foreigner, and its pretense at the same
time of doing so. Not being able really to understand,
and not being able to make itself understood, it has
thought that by increasing the number of policemen,
and the number of police investigations and police examinations, it must somehow make up for its inefficiency.
Hence the police system has by turn seemed ridiculous
or excessive, and it has been both. The official spy always
behind the palm of the Imperial Hotel, the police procura-
tor asking yards of questions, the absurd misunderstand-
ings of simple English words has made no end of humor
for the Tokyo visitor and the Tokyo reporter. That the
policeman has been the butt of such humor you need only
to pick up many a recent book on Japan to know. The
policeman did not read the book, but the chance is that he

did occasionally read the more easily read faces of the foreigners, and I can think of his satisfaction when war re-
leased him. It added at least one barb to his brutality. A
civilized Western nation would on that very account
have been only the more meticulously restrained, but the
Japanese is less civilized, and vengeance is quicker to him.
I have no doubt that the long-felt, long-suppressed, language annoyance enters generally into the explanation of
what has occurred—when small natures freed of law can
make up with blows for what they lack in understanding,
when they can pay back for years of not knowing what
the foreigner was saying. I think it undoubtedly contributed something to the plight of those many unfortunate
persons interned for months after the beginning of the war.

Language has been a definite part of Japan's isolation.
It has encased the mental and the political isolation. The
outside world has been shut out, because the amount of
Japanese language that the outside world has understood
has always been negligible. And the inside world has been
shut in. It must even have been a stimulus to a secret,
self-satisfying, flattering quality in the isolation, to have
the deaf ears of the world always right around. The language side of the national life has been practically a closed
chamber. Which accounts partly for the suddenness of
the nation's actions. The actions could be sudden because
all leaks from language could so easily be sealed in. The
suddenness has also been partly illusion, and dangerous

illusion, that the Japanese have been quick to capitalize.
It has helped them make themselves at certain moments
appear miraculous.

I remember a pleasanter side of the language problem.
As I have said, I never made any headway with Japanese.
But I did every late afternoon for a time, in a doctor's
house, sit on a pillow at the edge of his garden, so that
his young daughter might teach me. She had had three
years English in the middle school. She was a startling
diminutive person, looked as if she had come alive out of
on old print. There would be some English word she would
be trying to recall. She would narrow her narrow eyes,
press her thumb to her lips. "Ah—wis—wis—wistaria?
Yes? Wistaria?" The words would be so desperately
hard for her to find. To help herself she would shape
ideographs in large strokes on the air, then after a long
delay would blurt out something. "Purple flower?" "Summer time?" Three years of English in the middle school
simply would not reach. The garden was small, but toward
evening gave a feeling of great size, and as the light les-
sened gave that feeling more and more. She would see
me looking into the garden. She would look too. She
would try a long time, then burst out. "Pretty? Old
picture? Evening time?" Of course I would not have
needed one word of her inimitable English to grasp her
meaning, and I would tell her that the garden was majesti-
cal, poetical, and she would by the same process understand

me. I remember one evening how she startled me by whispering softly but right into my ear, "*Tsuki*." She pointed. The moon. *Tsuki*. The moon's name is gentle in all languages and never gentler than in the mouths of that girl's small sisters and brothers, who came presently and discovered, each with a tiny impulse of happiness, that *tsuki* had risen.

CHAPTER FORTY
They Imitate Everything

E VERYONE KNOWS HOW SHAMELESSLY THEY IMITATE.
They have in consequence of it seemed inferior. And, again,
in so far as our feeling at this point was precise, there was
no harm done us. But, again, in so far as it was not, it
resulted in an underestimating of their strength. Their
imitativeness is as gross as anything anyone ever says of
it. It runs from can labels to cannon. They even imitate
advertising copy. There is hardly a business house in
America cannot tell you some experience—twenty laundry
machines ordered by a Tokyo firm, one machine delivered,
the order for the other nineteen countermanded, and
presently laundry machines in exact imitation appearing
all over Japan. But what worries us now is that they,
notwithstanding, do very well in the war, and apparently
have not too entirely crippled their industrial capacity
by their continuous aping. It must make us suspect that
there was at least some straightness in their crooked
psychology. And this, I believe, was their complete lack of

sentimentality when they stole. They took bodily, and they took immorally, but they did not pretend to themselves that they were doing anything else. They did, of course, defend themselves to an American, but when they did they had almost to stop their ears from hearing what their mouths were saying. One explained that as soon as they read of an invention, but before they saw it, and before they knew even the principle, they "patented" the invention—and then worked it out completely on their own! Nevertheless, to themselves they have been, I believe, realistic. I doubt if they have, for instance, often made the common mistake of slightly modifying another's discovery and thinking they had the originality in themselves. That would have been much worse for them. That would have been much better for us. Theirs is a case of simple holdup. The state of mind is frank thievery. They have known where they stood. They have known what was not theirs. It is the advantage of seeing clearly. It makes the thief more dangerous. It keeps the inventive sides of his mind alive.

CHAPTER FORTY-ONE
It Must Be Remembered

THERE IS A CURIOUS ANCIENT JAPANESE WORD, *kunibiki*, meaning literally, country-pulling. It comes from a mythological story that Japan was once small, but that gradually it pulled over territory from Korea and became large. A little at a time. A little at a time. Japan will need to be carefully watched at the peace. Her history will need to be detailedly remembered. National characteristics only slowly change, and history is important in her case.

The lust for Asia is old. Korea was to be the stepping-stone. Hideyoshi's invasion came about three hundred and fifty years ago. He was not a cruel man apparently, yet he employed for this invasion a cruelty that the Koreans never forgave, started in them the lasting hatred they feel and have felt for the Japanese. He justified himself with the usual reasons. Korea was a closed country—he wanted it to be an open country. Korea had fought against Japan in the past—he wanted revenge for those ancient wars. Korea was near to Japan—in the hands of another power it was a threat to Japan. Korea was near to Japan—so it rightfully belonged to Japan. But what Hideyoshi really wanted was the highway to China.

The invasion failed. Japan sealed her ports. She rested—prepared—for three hundred years. Then her ports were forced open and she became, ostensibly, a modern nation.

Saigo was in favor of an immediate attack on Korea. So were Goto, Itagaki, many. Saigo had exact plans—plans that, they say in Satsuma, he was not allowed to use, but that were followed to the letter after he was dead. What the nation decided to do was to wait until it more effectively understood the West. Steadily, steadily, from that day to this Japan has improved her position in the world.

Toward China she took the attitude and never departed from it that China would continue a mass in flux and therefore subject to European nations, or would unite finally behind one strong man and become a neighbor of four hundred and fifty millions in competition with Japan's less than one hundred millions. Either outcome must be prevented.

The first long insistent bickering with China ended in the Sino-Japanese War. Japan decisively won the war. By the treaty she received Formosa and the Pescadores. China acknowledged the independence of Korea, and the Liaotung peninsula in southern Manchuria was ceded to Japan. So Japan apparently already had the steppingstone.

But Russia saw her chance of an all-year port on the Pacific thwarted, and the German Kaiser saw the yellow peril. France joined them. There was nothing for Japan to do but to give back the peninsula. China leased it to Russia—and Japan began instantly to prepare for war with Russia.

Ten years later the war came. Russia was beaten. Russia yielded her lease on the peninsula, also ceded her mining and railroad rights in South Manchuria. Both countries agreed to evacuate Manchuria—thus, though they were agreeing to Manchuria's independence, both really were clearing it for possible action of either. Korea was not annexed, but Japan's paramount position in Korea was recognized.

Again the people back home were exasperated. This time it was the indemnity—it was not large enough. And Korea had not been annexed. A chronic baiting began at once. Then, in August 1910, Korea was annexed. Now finally Japan did have the steppingstone.

The rest of the history every newspaper reader knows.

The lesson is plain. Japan may lose the present war, or may lose it in part, or win it in part. The treaty she makes may seem to block her. But it must be vividly remembered that she has been disappointed in the past, and has not been stopped—has insisted on getting everything that she has once set out to get. She would be quite able to swallow a defeat, I keep repeating—and go on from there. The peace must be thoughtful, the conditions wise, and Japan's vitality and insistence be constantly in our minds. And it must be daily remembered that we are not dealing with the international Japanese, or the Japanese of our big cities, full of small abortive movements of body, perpetually ingratiating, vulgarly clever, the successful tennis player, the successful small merchant. A nation of such— and this is still the picture of the Japanese in the majority of American minds—could never have brought the war even as far as it is now, could never have pursued a practically single policy through half a century, winning in the course of it three wars and numberless diplomatic campaigns. It is silly for us to have that small-town merchant in our minds. It is, in fact, offensive to us, because we would knock down a nation of him in a week's assault, as we sometimes foolishly thought we might do with the actual nation. There is something heavier, slower, more from the depths of the Orient, more mystically religious, more relentless, steadier, stubborner. This has representatives all over the nation, high and low, and these constitute the spine and brain. And these we can respect, must take the trouble to attempt to understand, and overcome.

CHAPTER FORTY-TWO
A Business Man

I MET THIS BUSINESS MAN IN THE FOLLOWING WAY. I was working on my biography of Noguchi. Wherever I ran on any Japanese who probably had figured in the story, I wrote him. No answer. I kept this up for about six months. Then one noon, just as I was starting for Albuquerque to learn something of Noguchi's studies of trachoma, I had a cable from Tokyo which read: "Please come to Japan. If you do I will pay half your expenses." The cable was signed Hajime Hoshi, a name I could not place, and the man could know nothing of me. But he did know that he was Noguchi's friend. So, instead of staying at Albuquerque, I sailed to Yokohama. Hajime Hoshi met me at the ship. He paid me the promised money in paper *yen*, a great stack of notes fresh from the bank. He took perfect care of me. He kept an automobile and a chauffeur in front of the Imperial Hotel all day and late into the night, and, though he was well past sixty, would drop in just as I was ready for bed, ask how my

day had gone, arrange the succeeding day, then hurry off
to his home which was a good distance, and be back to
talk to me the next morning while I was in my bath. He
had absolutely no nervousness. He went about Tokyo as
if it were a big country town. He conducted me up to
Wakamatsu, where Noguchi was born, and down to Kyoto
where one of Noguchi's friends had settled. I shall not
forget that friend. He had married a white woman, lived
with her up a gloomy short street, and after I had been
in the house a while she drew me over to her baby, looked
at it as if it frightened her, and I understood, for it was
dark and profoundly Japanese and already suggested
soldier. Poor woman. She had had a postcard from her
brother in America the preceding Christmas. She brought
it out and let me see.

On the train to Wakamatsu Mr. Hoshi peeled an apple
with a dagger-long pocket knife, stuck the knife into the
slices, put the first into my mouth, the second into the
mouth of his Japanese friend, the third into his own
mouth. At every station someone on the platform or
someone in the coach would recognize him, and he would
rise, and there would be a mumble-laden bowing. Back
once more in Tokyo, he arranged meetings for me with
as many as a dozen men a day, did it quietly and accurately,
some of the meetings with the most distinguished names
of scientific Japan, and yet he seemed always to have left
still a full day for his own business.. Finally, he deposited

me on the *Siberia Maru*, in the front cabin on the top
deck, introduced me to the Captain and the more distinguished passengers, put me in their personal care,
hurried down the gangway, and as the ship loosed her
moorings and slid off from the dock, lifted high a Japanese child, the first that came to hand, and the child
threw confetti.

Hoshi had come to the United States as a young man.
He had come to New York, studied at Columbia, graduated in 1901, started a newspaper, *Japan and America*,
and when the newspaper was on its feet, which took about
five years, he felt that he had done what there was to do
about that, sold it, returned to Japan. The newspaper he
started with $50, if I remember rightly, borrowed from
the Japanese Embassy.

In Japan he went into the drug business. He reasoned
it this way. Good drugs cure the sick, take away pain,
make the useless useful, help the Empire. "There is neither
frontier nor barrier to bar the spread of good medicine.
Besides, not only do medicines serve to cure diseases, but
act as their preventive." I think few would insist that
Hajime Hoshi is a great man, or an eminent man, and
he would not insist either. He is a business man, a manu-
facturer of drugs, who has had booming successes and
depressing reverses and noisesome court processes. He
often speaks of himself in the third person. "Hoshi come
to the top again. Hoshi a gambler. Hoshi does not care

for money. He make millions. He give millions away. He
do everything for Japan—the one country based on
Mother." And having thus worked around to his favorite
subject he is apt to grow vague and mystical—Japanese
do that, abruptly, as if something had cracked inside
them—say that all other nations are based on Father, the
Father who thinks primarily of present gain and advantage, whereas Mother is devotedly concerned with her
descendants, with things eternal, with the preservation of
the species, kindly, embracing, wanting nothing for herself,
her long life going back to Amaterasu, the Sun Goddess.
The talk now might run off on a most fantastic trail.
"Japan is teaching and caring for Korea with the heart
and mind of Mother. And is co-operating with Manchukuo
with the same maternal heart and mind. . . . This is possible
because Japan has no territorial design. Mother loves
another's child as she loves her own and aspires to better
and beautify other countries too in order to better the
world for her descendants to live in. This is the feeling
of Mother. Exactly the same feeling actuates Japan in
her relations and dealings with Formosa, Korea, and Manchukuo. . . . Biology shows that so far as mankind and
the feathered tribe are concerned, the male plays its part
in begetting and bringing up the little ones, but as for
other creatures, the female alone is responsible. . . . This
bare fact shows what the mind of Mother is. . . . There is
nothing to help progress except co-operation. Nothing

exists in the world except by co-operation. It should be considered therefore that co-operation is the motive power of progress dictated by God. . . . The Japanese people are a nation that observed the principle of progress and co-operation taught by the Sun Goddess, and the Japanese national policy itself is an incarnation of co-operation. Therefore domestic life, education, social life, politics, economic activities, and what not, in Japan are all based on co-operation. . . ."

I visited his factories outside of Tokyo. I shall never forget the long lines of bins containing the raw opium squeezed into balls, sent there from Persia, a guard watching over each bin, entering the bin in the morning naked, wearing a costume that always stayed in the bin, and leaving it in the evening naked, his cropped hair being subjected to special examination for the precious article. (Japanese pickpockets are the best in the world—the Japanese themselves say so. The most famous of them, the pickpocket of pickpockets, when caught was boiled to death.) There were floors and floors where morphine, cocaine, quinine sulphate, and half a dozen other major products for distribution throughout Asia, were in various stages of preparation, of packing, of shipping, or just being stored. His private office was a corner of one floor cut off with a crude board fence, nails in the fence to hang his hat and coat. Next the factory was the school where he gave lectures to his employees—on business method, Mother, world history, and Japan. "I established a Hoshi Pharmaceutical and Commercial School with a view to providing free education for the salesmen of my company and their youngsters and sons, even providing them with traveling, school, and all other expenses. On this account I dispersed several million *yen.* . . . I experienced the fact that even if one thinks of very good things, what he can think of is very much smaller than is actually possible." On the grounds, besides the Hoshi Company and the Hoshi School, was the Hoshi Bank, where the employees did their financial transactions, and the Hoshi Shrine, where the employees prayed.

Returning to this country I finished the manuscript of my book, and on the day I sent it to the publishers cabled the fact to Mr. Hoshi. That manuscript had cost him work and some hundreds of dollars. I had, of course, no answer to the cable. When the book was printed I sent a copy to him, and had no acknowledgment, so I sent a second copy, and no acknowledgment. I felt uneasy about this, convinced myself that I had said things in the book that were offensive to him, though I had not meant to, and there was nothing in any case that I could have done about that. After a half year I wrote him a note, and after another half year another note. Then one day I had a letter from a friend of his telling me Mr. Hoshi was bankrupt. He had gone by the side into the chainstore business, the first in Japan, and had failed. He was sued. In the court he made a fool of the judge, refused to give his name, or his age, generally refused, passed off everything with the fact that he kept nothing for himself, gave all to Japan. "This chainstore drug business of mine, however, was heavily impeded in its development by the occurrence of an unforeseen calamity. But I held my own and was able to overcome the difficulty. This proved possible solely because I had proceeded in the enterprise with the principle of Mother as my compass and carried out the principle that a business concern should allot one-fifth of its capital in personnel and four-fifths of it in things material. This would have proved impossible, however, had not Japan been a country created by Mother. All this I still continue to think over and over again with gratitude. For me, neither honor nor money is the object. I earnestly wish that the Japanese people, one and all, will understand the fact that Japan is a country created by Mother and will attain moral wisdom on the basis of this fact through intellectual rather than instinctive channels. I also wish that this fact be known and understood by all people in the world."

Four years after my book, without any word in the interval, I again had a cable from Tokyo, this one saying that Mr. Hoshi was on the way to Russia, would pass through the United States, through Chicago, would drop down to Cincinnati to shake hands with my mother and father, and that he would also go to Chile. He telephoned me when he arrived in San Francisco, telegraphed from

Chicago, reached Cincinnati, shook hands with my mother
and father, went on to New York, and I had no word for
another two years. I understood now his way of thinking
about it. One of the professors of our University, when
I introduced Mr. Hoshi to him, complained to him, said
that he had sent copies of a book of his to a dozen doctors
in Japan and never had an acknowledgment. Mr. Hoshi
seemed to wish to avoid discussing the point. He merely
made a few sounds. But the professor kept complaining.
Finally Mr. Hoshi said: "He could not write you a postcard of thanks, could he, and that way get done with the
obligation?"

I met him next in the Waldorf in New York. This was
the summer of 1937. He talked some of the "China incident." He said it would be settled soon. I asked him if he
meant that the fighting would be entirely over. "Oh no,
the fighting will go on, maybe ten years, maybe fifteen
years, maybe fifty, maybe a hundred. Sometimes there
will be more soldiers, sometimes there will be not so many,
maybe 10,000, maybe 50,000, always a handful, somewhere in Asia, when the Chinese do not behave." I asked
him how much of China he thought the Japanese troops
would occupy. "Oh, that depends. All the coast. Gradually
we will make business from there. We will not annex
China—oh no, we will not do that. We will only arrange
China so we can do business with China." Then he said
what his friend Prime Minister Hirota said before him:

"The world is three parts, Europe for the Europeans, America for the United States, Asia for Japan."

He received a reporter. He had on his dark blue belted coat. He had ripped the one pocket and had darned it himself with a coarse cord. His tie was not very carefully tied. His hair was a silky white. He wore silver rimmed specs. "I conduct business on the basis of kindness first, not only toward company but toward materials they use or handle. Be kind to yourself. Be kind to everybody. Be kind to your work. Be kind to materials you use. Be kind to money. . . . I say be kind to work. Barking dog is wiser than sleeping lion, popular saying in Japan. A brainy and able man is inferior to a dog if he neglects his duty. Many people live like sleeping lion. . . . Business grew. I made profit. Grew and grew. Now company capital seventeen million *yen* fully paid up. I own one quarter. We have 30,000 stockholders. These mostly independent drug store owners that sell my products."

Later he told me he wanted to make a gift to my city. He asked me how many cherry trees Washington had. I said I thought 3,000. He said he would give 5,000. I said that the Department of Agriculture would not let the trees in. He said he would grow them on Long Island. He said there were some growing there already, and the next morning left New York before dawn and was back at night. He said he wanted to show me some shoots. He also wanted to show them to the mayor of my city. I assured him that would not be necessary. He said the mayor might think the shoots just "small things." He had the shoots brought up into the room. They were saplings ten feet long. I tried to dissuade him from taking all those trees to Cincinnati. He said he must. I asked him whether he had a reservation on the train. He said, no, but that he would get one at the station. So, that afternoon, he and I and seven bags and the trees, like the forest of Dunsinane, went down through the great gaping lobbies of the Waldorf. The trees of course did not fit the taxi, so they were allowed to run up into the air out the window by the side of the driver—I do not know how he convinced the driver, but he was always free with dollar bills—and thus we went across midtown New York. I saw him as he was passing through the wicket towards the train—the ticket man possibly also convinced. I saw him again three days later in Cincinnati. I asked him whether he had had any inconveniences. He said, no. I asked him whether he had been able to get a stateroom. He said he had got an upper berth.

He wanted me to come again to Japan. I should come and stay a long time. I would be happy there. I could live—well, up on a mountain, if I liked to live on a mountain. He would find me a house. That would be easy. He would find me two servants, or three servants. Abruptly he had an idea, and it came out of him like a bursting discovery—I ought to take a Japanese wife. Yes, that would be best. And have Japanese children. That would be very good. Yes, I must do that. He kept painting the picture. He said how much more natural that would be, and how much better I would understand everything I saw. A wife—not a geisha—a wife would be much better. She could tell me stories. She could explain everything. He was utterly serious. He hardly for a moment questioned that the arrangement might be entirely satisfactory to me. He came back to it the next day, said it all over from the beginning, and then, I believe, rather took it that the point was settled.

And thus did Hajime Hoshi go limply around the world. I heard from him once since. He wrote that he had run for public office, had been elected, and would now be very busy with the Diet.

CHAPTER FORTY-THREE
Mitsuru Toyama, Fanatic

ONE OF HOSHI'S MANY FRIENDS IS TOYAMA, THE fanatic. Naturally Hoshi does not think him a fanatic. But to us Toyama is a fanatic, a dangerous one, and we dare not at all trust Hoshi's portrait, though there are strokes in it that should add to our idea of how a super-patriot may strike a very gentle Japanese, how he may sit like a Buddha in a revered corner of the Japanese mind. Toyama wears a white moustache, and a long pointed beard that looks as if it were tied on. I have known one American after another to see his photograph and say, "What a kind old gentleman!" And one said, "Santa Claus!"

In the United States Toyama would be an outlaw. It might take as long to trap him as it has certain superthugs, but I think it at least sure that he would not keep at large right down to his eighty-eighth birthday. Everybody in Japan knows of the assassinations Toyama has instigated, but no government agency dares or really cares to prove anything. A man like that is bound to have the honor of assassinations that he did not instigate, so Toyama's final murder list may be half as long or twice as long as the one he is credited with. Political murder list. Assassination on such a large and steady scale requires a large and steady fund. For this he has to be and is a master at extortion, huge sums, takes from the rich and gives to the poor, also takes from the rich and gives to the army. He has been in favor of the "liberation" of Korea, China, and the Philippines. It was Toyama founded the Black Dragon Society. This was before the China War. The Society was against foreign powers holding political rights in Japan, and in favor of war on China for the acquisition of Korea. It was because Okuma went slowly to the first end that he lost his leg with a bomb, and Toyama could not be convicted because the assassin who was delegated to the job hastily committed hara-kiri. Toyama is also credited with forcing Ito to agree to the Russian war or be assassinated. I doubt this. Toyama would have been capable of trying, but the evidence of character as against rumor is that Ito would have been capable of avoiding. It is said that Toyama initiated the war by ordering the undeclared attack on Port Arthur. He had his hand in Japan's action in China after the opening of the World War. He had his hand more recently in Manchuria. At the time of the London Naval Conference the Black Dragon Society is said to have promised that if the Japanese Commission agreed to the 5-5-3 ratio, all of them—including Yamamoto—would be assassinated. Yet, in spite of this record, Hoshi talked of Toyama as if he were an old piece of Satsuma china, frail and beautiful, that needed to be preserved from rough or unappreciative or even conceivably villainous hands. Hoshi always told me that if I would return to Japan I would have the privilege of writing Toyama's biography. I would be admitted to him. I would receive protection. (It would be interesting right now to have the data of that book.)

Toyama was born in 1855, two years after Perry, twelve years before the Revolution, twenty-two years before the Rebellion. Because he fought on the side of the rebels against the government he was jailed, but slipped out. He was born in the south. His people were unknown and poor. His boyhood hero was Hideyoshi, the warrior, and he began by modeling his life after that invader of Korea. His teacher was Saigo. In Kagoshima they told me how Toyama came to Saigo, asked to be his disciple, how Saigo said not a word, handed him a book. The book was "Cleaning the Mind and Heart," or "The Doctrine of Emptiness." (Essentially: Want nothing.) Toyama went with the book to the mountain. Stayed. Studied. Returned the book. And that was his whole training.

"Great man must occur here, then there, that is the law, that is the way all equals itself." (This was Hoshi speaking, and whenever he spoke of the superpatriot something

definitely hushed came into his voice.) "Toyama like
Saigo—they were friends. Saigo start the Rebellion, then
die—die twice, once when he swam out there in the sea
with the priest, and once when he commit *seppuku* after
he was wounded in the War of the Rebellion. Saigo end
with the Rebellion. Toyama go on, through the China
war, through the Russia war, through the Great War,
and through the China Incident." (This laudation of
Hoshi's was in 1937.) "Toyama show you the future. All
day Toyama sit there in his house, very still, hardly move
a finger." (Hoshi was sitting on a chair as he talked,
slipped, as a Japanese may, without a creak to the floor,
to show me how Toyama sat, looked like a Buddha in
pants, vest, and coat.) "Toyama was friend to Ito—no,
sometime friend, sometime enemy. When Ito try to push
through Constitution, Toyama does not like some parts—
so one after another members of Diet drop out of window
into branches of trees, so there is no quorum, then afterward spring back into window from branches again.
When Ito cannot make up his mind about the Russia war,
Toyama come—he come with four men into Ito's house,
does not say that he will kill Ito, just impress him that he
is the great man of Japan. You see? And then the war
begin.

"Toyama friend of Sun Yat-sen. Sun Yat-sen start the
China Republic in Toyama's house. Without Toyama,
no China Republic." (My God—I thought when I first

heard that—a Japanese superpatriot created the Chinese Republic, expecting, of course, to have China in a form easy to swallow at convenience.) "They have ideas, Toyama and Sun Yat-sen, the same kind. Sun Yat-sen get his from Toyama. Chiang Kai-shek—turn out not so good—get his from Toyama too." (Odd to realize that this is in a sense partly true.) "Sun Yat-sen saved by Toyama—flee to Toyama's house—from the tongs of the Emperors of China.

"Toyama different from Ghandi. Toyama does not go to the people, only speak to disciples, and the people come to him. Ghandi go to the people. Toyama hate war—but he will lift sword if necessary. He does not sit with hands folded. He say he hate war, but that the time is not yet. Co-operation is still on the war level. But he hate war, talk against it. He say, why cannot nations be competitors in humanity—why in guns. Toyama is right, Japan must make peace. The Mother, she must make peace." (Hoshi stopped, started again, expounded for a half hour his theme of Mother, and somehow got around, as Hirota would, as Toyama would, to a world divided into three parts, Europe, Asia, America, a Monroe Doctrine over each. Suddenly he concluded.) "Toyama not made one speech in fifty years." (The only speech he ever made was at the opening of the Hoshi school, and this Hoshi did not tell me.)

"Rioters and police run after East Indians in streets.

British Ambassador say East Indians must be arrested, cause trouble in China and India—but East Indians rush in Toyama's house. Toyama sit in door." (Hoshi showed me once more how Toyama sat.) "Rioters come from everywhere, fill street. Toyama sit in door. East Indians sit behind Toyama. Rioters in front. Rioters go away. Police come. Police know where East Indians are, but do not look. Police go away too.

"What is Toyama? That is hard to say. He learn from Saigo—he want nothing. That is the secret. Saigo had simple world to live in—so he is simple. No international problem. Toyama has international problem. Toyama only man living understand some things Saigo say—as sayings of Confucius can be understood only by certain men. So Toyama write book on Saigo, remarkable book. Toyama hold no office, he have no job, but where there is important work to do, there is Toyama." (When there is a leg to be blown off, as Okuma's in 1892, or a murder by soldiers, as Premier Inukai's in 1932.) "Where is the heart of Japan, there is Toyama. You point to him: That is Japan. He is looking after China. He is looking after India. He is looking after Ethiopia. When the Italians invade Ethiopia, Toyama send telegram to Selassie, and Selassie send telegram to Toyama." (In other words, Toyama is able to foresee, that were the Mediterranean to cease to be part British, it might begin to be all Italian, which it were well as early as possible to forestall. So

Toyama is sending a boost to Selassie.) "When Toyama get up from where he sit he walk very fast. Why does he walk fast? Because when he was boy he walk sometimes fifty-sixty miles a day. No one can keep up with Toyama. Big man. Many geisha his friends. Many love letters—I see once, in his house. Eat very little, no meat, no fish, sometimes only leaves. On New Year Day Toyama call on nobody, only two, the Emperor and the Lord of his clan. Then he go home and sit again. Where Lord of clan has great teacher-philosopher like that, clan is leader."

Abruptly it occurred to me, and I asked, and was surprised to learn that Toyama had a wife—he squatted there such a solitary—a wife twenty years younger, and "about" five children.

CHAPTER FORTY-FOUR
The National Religion Is Shinto

ADMIRAL TOGO WAS ASKED WHY HE HAD SELECTED Tsushima Straits to engage the Russian fleet, and he answered that it was there that the ships of Kublai Khan, about to attack Japan, had been scattered, and that he expected the ghosts of the Japanese soldiers of that day to come and do battle with the living Japanese soldiers of this. On that occasion the ghosts seem to have been most helpful. And ghosts generally are believed to take part in Japanese life. The dead keep functioning with the living. Originally the gods of the sun and moon were born on earth—in Japan, that is—and only later went up into the sky. The two dominant Japanese religions have always been important to the nation in war, for they are the kind that can be bent to war. Our religions, on the contrary, are more apt to start debates of conscience when war comes. Indeed, Japan's most ancient religion is a positive incitement to valor in war, to indifference to death, to intensity of patriotism, a natural religion for a despotism—not that a despotism would have to follow—and a natural religion also for both victory and defeat, because victory becomes but the step to further victory, and defeat is merely an interlude.

But there is no doubt that the Japanese are a religious people. The three principal religions are Shinto, Buddhism, and then, after a good distance, Christianity. Confucianism is an ethics rather than a religion. Each of the three is separate by definition, but there is usually more than one of them behind the life of any individual Japanese, and it would not be easy to say where one began and another ended. I recall the torment of an American woman, a Methodist missionary, who had been in Japan for years, and said that just as the Japanese had more or less fused Buddhism and Shinto, she felt that now they were trying to fuse Christianity with the other two, and this to her meant the defilement and denial of the true faith. The ordinary Japanese, not too differently from ourselves, makes up his everyday religion from the beliefs around him, and does not try to define them too clearly. But those beliefs do have much more concreteness than religious beliefs in modern Europe and America. Hoshi says, "The Japanese worship gods as ancestors daily and create gods as descendants daily too." The dead, from whom the living come, are the gods of the living, and the living will die and be the gods of the living who are to come. Ghostly past and ghostly future make one fabric. Where the emphasis is toward ancestry, it is Shinto, and where the emphasis is toward eternal return, it is Buddhism. Hoshi says, "The words heaven and god connote ancestry, and to the Japanese the three are practically one and the same."

The native religion and the most ancient is Shinto. There are many forms of Shinto—deities of rice fields, of food, of trees, of rivers, of wind, of clan. There are shrines to statesmen. One of the most visited is that to General Nogi, who with his wife committed the double hara-kiri. At the famous pottery in Satsuma when they sealed up the kiln they prayed to the deity of kilns—did that while I was there—and declared the day a holiday. To us at present the most important of the forms of Shinto is the worship of the Imperial ancestry. It is the most powerful, the most surviving, and, naturally, the most nourished of all the cults. Everyone subscribes to this as an expression of his patriotism, whatever his religion.

I was with the surgeon in whose house I had stayed that first night in Satsuma. Before us was a Shinto shrine standing in the hot Kagoshima sun. There are several hundred thousand such Shinto shrines in Japan. He was showing me the shrine.

A woman came, left. Another woman. Then a woman with a boy by the hand. She approached the shrine over a broad gravel walk with old trees on either side. The walk in the great shrines is as suggestive of august destination as anything in this world, and sometimes this may be so in even a poor village shrine. The woman continued all the way up to the shrine, dropped to her knees, clapped her hands, left an offering of a few kernels of rice, several times bent her body so that her forehead touched the earth, then got briskly up, took her boy by the hand, walked away. She had perhaps prayed to a good many gods unitedly. She may specifically have mentioned the great national gods, the local gods, and her own household gods. This woman's grandfather was perhaps a samurai, because the masses, who support the Government with taxes, are Buddhist.

The shrine was a trim, inconspicuous structure, raw wood, no paint, carefully preserved and watched over, some cuttings of white paper hanging from above and indicating the number of the ghostly gods. Within, it was as empty as most Japanese structures. I watched the priest go through his rigorously prescribed movements. The shrine had a clean-washed look and, though the day was hot, it left over me a cool feeling.

There was that coolness also around this surgeon's family—the old woman, the wife, the surgeon, the children, and it seemed to go out even into the servants. Cool but unyielding. Not swayed by sentimental storm. I am told that when the surgeon was young he was a great drunkard, overnight gave up both drinking and smoking. Shinto disciples often drink, and also often thus suddenly reform, and you get the feeling that they indulge for the discipline of breaking through the indulgence. Everyone in that surgeon's family believed unswervingly in the divinity of the Emperor, and admitted the right of his dominion over each one of their private lives. Everyone in that family accepted the idea of the divine origin also of the Japanese race, hence its superiority.

The surgeon had been talking to me while the two women prayed, now stopped, went up to the shrine, and himself prayed. When he returned he said that his family came regularly to this shrine. Of course, they had also their small shrine at home, where they prayed several times each day and left offerings of *sake* and rice. I asked him whether there was not some admixture of Buddhism in his religious feeling, and he said no. He was a severe man but a just one. His boy was with us. I asked what the boy would do when he grew up. "He will be a surgeon, like his father, unless there are signs that the nation is in trouble, then he will be a soldier." The father said this quietly, and the son listened quietly, and I knew that the future would be just that way. Once in the year each child in that family decided how many rice balls he wanted to eat at a meal—one, two, or three—and what was decided was the rule for the year. No more and no less would be eaten. This rule, the father said, was part of their religion, and I believe it. The servants were not subject to the rule, exactly because the rule was not for economy but for religion. The father instructed his son that even if he was hungry, and even if he was asked twenty times, and even if he was hungrier and hungrier, he must keep saying that he had had his dinner. To do otherwise was bad manners. And bad religion. The samurai even if he had not eaten for days, gestured with his toothpick.

I remember the night I finally left the surgeon's house. I had been away in the town to make some last arrangements, returned by rikisha, the runner taking me right through the bamboo gate in the bamboo fence, and there, much as if a curtain had been lifted on a stage, knelt the entire family—the old woman, the wife, the husband, the children, the servants. They were waiting for me. They bowed to me in unison. They were saying farewell. And there was some kind of strength of feeling there—a religious feeling, I believe—that may have been Shinto.

CHAPTER FORTY-FIVE
A Christian

THE RIKISHA TOOK ME TO THE RAILROAD STATION. IT was by now after ten o'clock at night. It had begun to rain, and I had my luggage below me at my feet and an oil-paper umbrella unsteadily over my head. I was expecting no one at the station, was picking my way through the usual crowd, when a graying gentleman with a youthful stride came hurrying. He was the old doctor—the one whose skinny boy had escorted me up Kirishima mountain. The old doctor was looking for me. He was still on his working day, had seen patients from early morning, had just come from one, would go on to another. He was a highly respected citizen of the town and everyone made room for him, was perhaps the best known physician, certainly the best known Christian. That last was written on him. He was a man who had seen suffering, and had taken part in the suffering he had seen. He was born different from anyone in the crowd, but his religion also made him different, permeated his nature, even his body, a gentle body that it made gentler. This all was further emphasized by his coming in kimono. He was a sincere and a devout man. He could not have been Shinto. He could, I suppose, have been Buddhist, though his simple friendliness toward every creature that he touched—even those whom he did not know right there in that crowd—would then have been less expressed.

He had brought me a gift. He ripped the colored cord and the colored wrappings off of it, unfurled it as he might an important document, though really it was only a panorama photograph of his city. He presented it to me, and it was as if he were presenting me the city. He was himself completely a piece of the city, so that it even surprised me somewhat when I asked him, and he answered that he had studied at the Imperial University.

I had visited him several times in his clinic. He called it clinic and it had the quality of clinic, made one think of a Florentine market place where the ill congregate. Many people. All classes. Actually it was his private practice. The clogs stood out in a row, not as many as at the theater, but many. The building was inside a fenced yard, a big waiting room with three walls open, the patients, after they had taken off their clogs, stepping up onto the veranda, then kneeling singly or in small groups here and there on the *tatami*. Along one side was a narrow bench, and on this, where we should expect people to sit, people kneeled. Once when I was there the doctor had his own recently born baby lying on a blanket on the floor, protected by a mosquito netting. It was huge for a Japanese baby. He said that it was three months old and that it would be his last, and he laughed. He said that he had had many, and he laughed again. This one was by his second wife, a woman whom I would have judged forty, and who was known in Kagoshima for her many Christian activities. He said that he himself was more than eighty.

He was close friends with the principal Christian missionary of the city, a spinsterish woman. I myself would not have found it easy to be friends with her. She had, as we say, a good heart, and she had a piano, and she kept unfortunate children in her ugly small house, and she taught them to sing Christian songs. But her life down there in the south had been a hard uphill deforming fight, the world around her never really with her, laughing at her often, sarcastic to her often, sometimes brutally contemptuous. The Shinto doctor, for instance, hated her, and when he bowed to her it was with Shinto cold. "She spends her strength making women's skirts longer." Very possibly she had been too insistent that she had inside her the whole immortal truth, had brought it along with her, and did not consider that Buddhism and Shinto, that had made this nation, must have values in them also. But the old doctor was her steady good friend. He saw Christ through her.

Christianity came to Japan by way of Satsuma. St.

Francis Xavier had been in India, had converted a Japanese, who had returned home, whereupon St. Francis was invited by the Lord of Satsuma to come to Kagoshima, and stayed three years. This was in 1552. By 1581, twenty-nine years, there were 150,000 converts and 200 churches. Hideyoshi, the warrior, began to oppose the new religion. His immediate successors increasingly opposed it. The number of converts meanwhile had increased to 600,000. Then the killing began, Christians losing their lives often by the cruelest tortures. Nevertheless the religion survived. Believers would pretend not to believe, missionaries would hide, and continue also to slip in with the foreign ships, which became one of the reasons for the final sealing of the ports.

There is a simple story of those days. A Japanese girl was caught by the spirit of the new religion. When it came time for the baptism she asked again what were the rewards? She was told that she would go to heaven. This was very satisfying to her. But then it occurred to her that she would like to make sure also about the fate of her mother and father. She was told that they, being pagan, would not go to heaven. She decided that she would have to reconsider. If she were Buddhist or Shinto, or some of both, she would die and she would be among her ancestors, and her mother and her father would be there. But if she were Christian and would die, she would go to heaven all alone.

There are many Christians in Satsuma. I knew a number of devout Christian doctors. And I knew devout Shinto and Buddhist doctors, some of whom received their education in America or Europe. On the whole these latter avoided any talk that led toward their household gods, or toward their actual belief in the divinity of Hirohito, though several times there was also a surprisingly frank avowal of their belief. They seemed different from the Western scientist, who is apt to be a skeptic, or his religion is apt to be the kind that feels called upon to prove the closeness of science and religion. To us religion has become generally more impersonal. To the Japanese it is still very personal. Or so it seemed to me.

I shall always remember a missionary on a ship returning from Japan. He was a big-bodied man, dark-skinned from having been much out of doors, a broken look, or a look of being out-at-the-heels without really being that, whitening hair, too old for someone that young. I fell into talk with him. He had come to Japan seventeen years before, fresh from college, full of the zeal to spread his faith. In his area the converted did not smoke, did not drink, and if they were school children did not even study on the Sabbath, but only read the Bible and interpreted. He kept them naively earnest, as indeed they were inclined to be—encouraged them in that direction partly for the example. After some years he began to suspect that all was not as it seemed, so labored with even greater zeal.

He grew discouraged. For a time he still managed to cheer himself with the usual thought that where everything was so very different, his work might yet come out all right. At last he could conceal from himself no longer that the Japanese around him were coming to him largely for things, not faith. They wanted what he could give to them. Gifts from the home church in America, exercise in the English language. He ought to go home, but he had invested so much of his youth, so he stayed. Finally came the decision of the Japanese authorities to center all power in the church in Tokyo, whose officers were entirely Japanese. Henceforth all money contributed by Americans would be distributed by Japanese, which convinced him at last that the Japanese were using the Christian church only for their own material and national ends. The money would drop into the Japanese church and there disappear. Might even be used to buy American scrap iron and oil. So he was returning home. He felt his life was done. He felt he was too old to begin anywhere new—thirty-eight. He felt he had spent his life in fostering a mammoth hypocrisy. He passionately predicted the day—which did of course come—when the Japanese would openly drive against Christian missions, schools, and all foreign organizations. He thought there would be horrible killings again as in the years after Hideyoshi.

But the eighty-year-old Christian doctor with his young wife and his many children and his huge baby, was no hypocrite. He was one of those people who can see one God, and can see all people as one people, and there are not many human beings anywhere who are able honestly to do that.

CHAPTER FORTY-SIX
A Buddhist Dies

BUDDHISM WAS DISESTABLISHED IN 1871. IT HAD GONE side by side with Shinto for a thousand years. Henceforth Shinto was to stand alone as the religion of the state.

The old Grandmother at Funakura told how it was in Satsuma just after 1871. She remained, of course, Buddhist. Most everybody in the village remained Buddhist. And no one much troubled them. Now and then when the Shinto officials wanted money, the Buddhists were fined for being Buddhists, as a way of raising the money. That is, it was impossible to stamp out Buddhism, but by making it illegal, if the government needed money it could start a raid and collect. But it never came to much. Once the Funakura family had a bit of manure. Valuable! So they spread it over the edge of the field of the Lord of Satsuma—and were fined because they were Buddhists trespassing. But the manure was allowed to remain.

And now and then their small images, their Buddhas, might be seized and buried. The owners would be sorry but there was nothing they could do. The old woman across the street, Grandmother's friend, was one who had had her Buddha stolen. Sometime later in her sleep she dreamed of a six-way Buddha—one arm to the East, one to the West, one to the North, one to the South, one down toward the earth, one up toward the sky. She dreamed that the image was buried in the graveyard. So she got up in the dark, and there was just the first streak of dawn when she arrived at the graveyard. Looked for the grave. With a small blade dug into it, several feet. Found the image. Their house, she said, had for a long time before that been on the decline, but its fortunes now immediately rose.

Grandmother herself had had a dream. In it Buddha said to her: "There is a small image, a Buddha, with peculiar eyes—see that it is properly placed." And Buddha also told her the house. She waked. She went. The people of that house were not Buddhists. They were just saying that they knew nothing of any image when the maid interrupted, said there had been an old package lying about, had come from Tokyo. The image was in the package, of course. And, of course, also had the peculiar eyes. The family immediately became Buddhists. Even Grandmother's husband, the man of the two *tatami*, was rather impressed by this. And Funakura was impressed—Buddha coming to her and talking to her in her sleep.

Grandmother's religion was real and it was formal. I

saw her many times every day go to the corner in the room where the shrine stood, bend her head, close her eyes. I do not suppose she would have known if some Shinto had got mixed up with her Buddhism.

Buddhism was introduced from Korea about the middle of the sixth century. It brought the idea of kindliness. The Buddhist priests of the early period seem to have been wise. They did not set up the new religion in opposition to the old, rather let it run side by side. It came as an ally. There is so much in all religions that is and must be the same, that it was possible to point out the samenesses, explain that only the names of things were different, and thus make it easier for the convert to come along without undue violence to his past.

The Japanese repeat: "Shinto is like the root and stem, Confucianism like the leaves, Buddhism like the seed and flower." The Buddhist priests taught that one's misfortunes in this life were the punishment for bad deeds in past lives, one's good fortunes the reward for good deeds, which made it profitable to be good instead of bad in the present life. The ghost world of Shinto was redefined, but it was not torn away. It would simply have been impossible to tear away the ancestors—would be impossible today. Buddhism discouraged individuality. The individual was to melt his will, his desires, his hopes, into the universal. He came from eternal combination and recombination. He was an aggregation, an accidental meeting of past fragments, and when he died, what he would become would be fragments of countless futures. The nearest such universal around him that the living Japanese could see was, of course, his nation. To people anywhere, their own country is best, is right, is just. To the Japanese also. But to the Japanese with their long discipline in Buddhism it is comparatively natural for the individual to identify himself with the nation, move where it moves, float wherever that total of forces happens to be pushing the single one, and to do all this without any internal reservation. They speak of the carpet of life. The fabric of life. These expressions apply especially to Buddhisms. And the mind that lies behind them is at this moment a potent part of the military power of the nation.

The Funakura Grandmother was weakening and it was certain that she could not live much longer. She lay over toward the garden. It was cooler there. Just one blanket had been rolled out along the floor. They wanted to bring her a cloth pillow. She would not hear of it. She had had a lifetime of practice sleeping "hard." Her son and her grandson squatted one to either side of her. The son was the second son, the eldest was himself ill, so sent his eldest, now head of the house, to represent him. And the Funakura grandmother's youngest was too far away to come. Now and then one or the other, son or grandson, took hold of her parched yellow hand. She would doze. She would wake, would say that she must have been sleep-

ing. It looked like evening—was it evening? Or was it
morning? She said she was losing all track. She said she
knew she was going to die. She did not mind at all. The
three talked of everything. The house, of course, would
go to Ichiro, the oldest. He ought to have the roof tiled.
He would not have enough money for that. So the other
two must help him. If they did not have the money right
now, they could borrow it from the banker—the banker
was stingy, but he was vain, and if they would just talk
to him of his brother who had been elected last year to
the Diet, he would loan them any amount. But after he
had loaned them the money, they must spend it at once,
because if he had a chance to think it over he would surely
want it back.

The old doctor, the Christian, came to see her. She was
a Buddhist. He was a Christian. The son and the grandson did not know what they were. All had been friends
for many years. The old doctor recognized that he could
not help her. She did not want to be helped. She was
anxious for what would happen next—talked of it as
matter-of-fact as of a bargain at the expense of the huck-
ster. About the process of dying she was negative—but
she very definitely wanted to go. The old doctor told her
that everyone in Funakura was speaking of her, was learning from her example. They were saying that all her sons
were dutiful and that she had deserved dutiful sons. And
she answered: that Buddha had seen to it that she had had

dutiful sons, that Buddha had never let anything wrong come to her. Poverty was no wrong. It was her husband who had suffered the pain of poverty. He was Confucian. Presently her thoughts turned once more to the son who could not be there. As soon as she was dead the oldest was to write to him, was to tell him all about it, how easy it had been, and they were to send him 200 *yen* for his children. "Yes, write to Kaio as soon as it is over, tell him everything." She lapsed into unconsciousness. A telegram came. There was no slightest noise. Yet she waked. The telegram was from the youngest—he was sending money to them! Money! She smiled. She lapsed.

Her second son took her one hand. Her grandson took the other. They wet her lips with tea. She died. In the room it was yet stiller than usual. The old doctor said: "She who just died was a remarkable Christian."

CHAPTER FORTY-SEVEN
Where Is the Center?

Tʜᴇ ᴊᴀᴘᴀɴᴇsᴇ ʜᴀᴠᴇ ᴀ ᴘʀᴏᴠᴇʀʙ, "ɴᴏ ɢʀᴇᴀᴛᴇʀ ꜰᴏᴏʟ than he who has power and talks of it." They talk constantly of their Emperor. So the chance is that the center of power of the nation is not in the Emperor. Where is it? That is not easy to answer. Not for any nation. And most difficult for Japan. The foregoing chapters make it possible, and interesting, at least to discuss the point.

To begin with, I have always been sure that the prattle of Japanese political parties, the courtroom speeches of patriot assassins, the mouthings of military demagogues, or of the peace-on-earth purring internationalists, the coups, the cabinet crises, that all that up-and-down was but the battle of boys in the back yard. When papa looked out the window and nodded that there should be an end to it, the boys would unite, fall into line, and go where they were told. But who then is papa? Or, to put it differently, it is often as if a finger pointed and commanded: Do this. But whose finger? An assassin feels the urge to assassinate. A prime minister feels the urge to resign. A prominent war minister feels the urge to depart for an obscure post in Manchuria? Whose is the finger?

The Japanese throughout their history have kept the seat of power unemphasized. They do not necessarily conceal the truth from themselves, but concealment is in their nature. And it is in their nature also to be satisfied with the substance and to surrender the shadow. From 1192 to 1867 the Emperor was the Emperor, but the Shogun was the power. That is, the Japanese could for six and three-quarter centuries lay aside their Emperor. The line had lost its vitality, so the Shoguns took hold, but did not disturb the form of goverment, and the line could come back when the vitality came back. During one hundred and thirty-four years of those six and three-quarter centuries, it was not the Shogun but his regent who had the power. Which left the Emperor the shadow of the shadow of the substance. But the quintessence came when there was a regent for the regent. The shadow of the shadow of the shadow. It shows how Japanese the Japanese can be. It is an important piece of history to remember. It is an important piece of the Japanese mind. It throws light on many things—on a period of years just recently when the Japanese let the world go on thinking that their armies had bogged down in China. And they would allow us a victory in the present war if they could see that their defeat had in it the substance of the future.

Where is the center of power? The Emperor is an idea and a man. It is that way in Britain. The idea has the power, the man has little. Yet the loyalty of the Japanese to the Emperor is as strong and personal a feeling as we have in any country in the world today. Ito advised his son that the first fact of life was to be loyal to the Emperor. The utterly different, unemotional, undramatic, Yamagata said that he would be willing to die at any time for the Emperor, and of course he meant it. Japanese soldiers are dying everywhere now, and doubtless many of them are saying to themselves in the last conscious moment, that it is for the Emperor. Yet all power is out of those Imperial hands. The power is always diffuse and somewhere else, and the Emperor is only the symbol. As a person the Emperor is an inconspicuous, apparently pleasant, modest, forty-one-year-old man, with an amateur professor's interest in biology. We may be very sure that he is not being retired by the militarists, for that is not necessary. His father—in whom also it would have to be said that the power resided—was for most of his Imperial career a helpless mental invalid. And his grandfather, the great Meiji, was remarkable for the way he could let the men around him rule undisturbed. Yet the Emperor is the "sacred person," and where he intrudes he is never disobeyed—but where he intrudes there is almost never an issue. The issue is already settled. He is kept away from the sordid, the day-to-day, the factual. The center of power is not in him.

And not in the political parties. The party system throughout its entire history has been near to ridiculous. The Japanese have no idea what a truly functioning party system means. They have read of it. They have dabbled in it. Certainly the power has never been there.

And the power is plainly not in the individual voting citizen, not in the people, at least not in that sense. They know no more what to do with the franchise than they know what to do with the party. They did not want the franchise to begin with, did not demand it, have had it only nominally, have always had it hamstrung by restrictions. The franchise is a farce. It was a farce also in the liberal twenties. Nothing of importance in Japanese government has yet been so concretely and so frankly stated as to be settled by the yes or no of the ballot. Power is vague in Japan, and more dangerous.

Is the power in a leader? There is a Hitler in Germany. A Mussolini in Italy. There was a Napoleon in France. A Caesar in Rome. No one could possibly say that there was any such leader in recent history in Japan. In almost every country in the contemporary world we can name a man who is stronger in power and longer in power than any living Japanese. Until the war began we could not even remember the names of the leaders. And the power passed from hand to hand till it gave us the impression that there were nothing but mediocrities in the nation. In the last one hundred years of history, even with all the gallery of strong men, there has never been a concentration of total power in one man. Saigo never got outside of Satsuma, his clan. Ito was a truly international figure, visible, human, and yet he hardly achieved a single lasting thing except as he won advantages for Japan from the foreigner. Yamagata had power, to get done a certain piece of work, very limited, very important to the nation, because the army has been important to the nation, but what is most striking about him almost is his lack of individualism, his bleak embodiment of a will not in himself but in the emerging modern Japan. Toyama has power —rather, had it, for he is a very old man, and the violence that he represents has gone on after him, was before him, and is plainly always a young fact in Japan. He was the embodiment of that. Hoshi was no doubt right when he said: "Toyama is Japan." Except that the statement would need some modification like: Toyama was Japan at that time.

Is the power in a small violent clique? Is it in a limited band of fanatics? A gang? That is what we are inclined to believe. That is how it superficially looks. I have already expressed my doubt of this, and pointed to the danger for us in believing it if it is not true. Some equivalent of gang action has been the normal process of Japanese history, and the gang in that sense is not new to contemporary Japan. But the personalities in the Japanese gang keep changing, so it certainly has not the character of a small violent clique grabbing power. Violence is rather the nation's way of settling affairs. Assassination, murder, intrigue, suicide, rebellion, war, have been the methods. In the West that was often true also, but centuries ago. Japan is still back in those old centuries. It is settling affairs as it has always settled them. Even the peace-loving Ito got to his first ends by violence. Violence was the history of the nation before the Shogunate, and during the Shogunate, and since. It is today. The number and the memberships of the so-called superpatriot societies is so great that that alone ought to make us hesitate over the idea of small cliques. In very recent years it has been the "Manchuria Gang," which was almost from the beginning as large as an army, ramified and ramified, till it includes now the whole Japanese nation. This is the normal Japanese evolution. And the way the personnel of the so-called Younger Officers' Group, the war parties, the war cabinets, et cetera, have shifted year on year and month on month ought to make us realize that no gang drove Japan into war. It was rather a gang nation that went to war.

Is there a plan for the gang nation? Obviously. Has there always been a plan? Obviously. From long before the Restoration. Korea was the steppingstone. Again and again the Japanese tried to establish that steppingstone. Long before Hideyoshi. But it had to be established across water, and when modern warfare alone made that possible, that steppingstone was established with the slowest most exacting care. Saigo was not allowed to attempt it because the nation did not yet feel strong enough. The Sino-Japanese War attempted it but could not complete it. The Russo-Japanese War practically completed it. Ito stood in the way of the completion. He was assassinated. The Great War took on the adjoining German territory. The steppingstone was firm now. Korea, China, and beyond, was the plan—the beyond perhaps somewhat vague. But generally speaking, it was yellow against white, a Japanized Asia against the world. A document like the Tanaka Memorial is of small interest, except that it states more or less candidly a nation-wide, history-long, scheme. That particular statement leaked out because of one blundering fool, or he was instructed to put it out as international bait. And it must be grasped that for a plan of such dimension the nation could well afford to wait on through victories and defeats.

Where is the center of power?

I believe that the difficulty in defining it is that it is not at one point, but that it is somehow in the total nation. It is diffuse, and always only apparently moving in the direction of the momently strongest part of the nation. The Japanese speak of their "destiny." To us that is a distasteful idea because we feel immediately the dishonesty in it. It is putting the burden on fate, which automatically makes everyone who opposes it wrong. Yet all nations do have a destiny to a degree. In their physically upsurging periods they try to realize it through action. In their physically declining periods through philosophic statement. For three-quarters of a century the Japanese have had somewhat more reason than other nations to believe in the stark reality of that destiny. Furthermore, Japan is more single-minded with its destiny than any other nation. That is because Japanese easily feel and act as a total. The Japanese are still essentially a clan. The Restoration was simply a coalescence of the clans into one large clan. The clan instinct remains. It is what one senses in every Japanese house, over every charcoal burner, every tobacco *bon*, in a Forty-seven-Ronin-reading assembly, in a school. In Funakura a man told me that the greatest horror to a Japanese is that he might tarnish his family, and after that his clan, and after that his nation. He dreads this more than anything that touches him personally. And "dread" was the word the man used. The individual is willing to lose himself in the mass, and the mass still ferments as a total. It is a self-contained total, self-absorbed, takes its own counsels exclusively, has looked at itself so steadfastly that of the West it really knows only the surfaces. Nothing was ever more farcical than the dapper, all-present, fraternizing, international familiarity of the Japanese at Geneva in the early days of the League. You needed only to see that not to believe in it. I had a long talk with Matsudaira while he was Ambassador to England and daily in touch with Geneva, and I shall never forget, for all his man-of-the-world quality, how essentially remote as a Buddha he sat in his high-walled London rooms.

And what is it makes it possible that a center of power can run thus through a nation? I believe it is because this nation always was and still is isolated. It has the oneness of isolation. The present isolation, which is a quality of mind, extends directly back into the physical isolation before 1853, and that goes back into the ancient isolation of the family and the clan. Isolation has been one continuous piece. The fact that the nation has lived on an island has helped. Were Japan truly to become an Empire, if that were possible, the isolation would, of course, slowly disappear. The feeling toward the foreigner has always been and is remote. The feeling toward the foreigner has always been and is inflexible. Which partly accounts also for the cruelty. Wherever the foreigner is concerned the Japanese minds move together. The nightly talk in the millions of homes, in the thousands upon thousands of geisha houses, the daily prayers at the hundreds of thousands of Shinto temples, are still concentrated on Japan, not mankind. For no other of the great nations is that so. Japan has a solitariness that is an anachronism in the modern world, that will be impossible in the future, and that, were it not dispelled in any other way, would be dispelled by the advance of the machine.

I am afraid it will be only after we have forced and wooed Japan out into the world, not by a war alone but by long years of intelligent peace, that we shall be able to place the center of Japan's power at a tangible responsible point, where we can negotiate with it, talk with it, meet it in conference, compel it to compel its leaders—and its people—to consider the needs of the entire world.

CHAPTER FORTY-EIGHT
The President of the Bank of Japan

ON MY FIRST VISIT TO JAPAN I CARRIED WITH ME a piece of pottery. The pottery was to be a gift from the President of my University to the President of the Bank of Japan. These two men had been classmates at Ann Arbor. A Japanese doctor escorted me to the bank. We were shown to the President's room—a bulky imitation of the room of an American board of directors. The President stood up. The President bowed. I was struck at once by the way he ignored the doctor, did not invite him in, just let him stand, till finally the man went and sat in a chair that was outside the door. Class remains class. I presented the vase. I needed to say a few words, could not immediately think of any, then asked the President whether his path had ever crossed Lafcadio Hearn's. "Oh yes," he said, "my son is right now studying in the middle school where he is taught by Hearn's son." Then abruptly he laughed, a belly laugh. Did I know the great joke played on Hearn?

It ought to be emphasized, what everyone outside of

Japan realizes, that Hearn did more for the Japanese than any million *yen* of propaganda they ever spent, because Hearn wrote so that he was read all over the English-speaking world, was translated, and is more responsible than anyone else for the idea of the Japanese as a people of great delicacy, gentleness, and grace.

The President of the Bank of Japan recovered from his laughter, then went on to say that Hearn had been under contract to the school where he taught English, earning about three times as much as a native professor. I might explain that Hearn would need to earn that much, because he would need to buy foreign foods which were expensive, would need glass windows in his house, and a stove. He was frail, never well, always cold. The President continued, that as time went along Hearn had more and more identified himself with the Japanese. Finally his patriotism—his pro-Japanese patriotism—was so compelling that he simply must apply for Japanese citizenship. He applied. He got his papers—and the next morning found his salary cut to one-third! For was he not now a *Japanese* professor!

That was the great joke. The President of the Bank of Japan laughed noisily. I do not know if the facts about Hearn are true, but it makes no difference. The point is that this trick of the Japanese government was the President's idea of a huge practical joke. And what was more amazing was that the President of the Bank of Japan should so slightly understand an American as to think that that story must seem very funny to me too.

We usually say that the Japanese have no sense of humor. Perhaps. That they do not have a sense of our humor is, of course, true. But a sharp appetite for a practical joke, even the most extraordinary kind, they do have. And that is a fact for us always to remember.

On that first visit to Japan I had been advised to take along certain foods, therefore had fitted the bottom of one of my trunks with a row of cans containing flour, sugar, coffee, salt, allspice, and above the cans had hung two hams and a bacon. A committee of doctors met me at the pier, assured me that I need not bother to go through the customs with my trunks, that these would arrive safely at the hotel. They did. The salt was mixed with the flour, the sugar with the coffee, everything spilled out, thrown together, neatly poured back. I have no way of being sure that this did not occur accidentally—but it did occur on that morning of the day the American Exclusion Act went into effect. I was disposed to swallow the explanation of the doctors, that some idiot customs officer had not known one Western food from another. When, however, my two hams and the bacon were hung under the eaves of a Tokyo house to keep them cool, and after a few hours were represented by three strings with the pieces of skin attached, and it was explained that hungry dogs had come and eaten the meat, I knew the

Conclusion

WE AMERICANS HAVE LAID OUT A DIFFICULT TASK for ourselves. We shall have to beat the Japanese, build up a vast machinery of war to do it, toughen our sensibilities to do it, die to do it, kill to do it, and then when it is done, look at them, and their minds, and their daily life, and their national life, and the future, all, with caution, knowledge, imagination, and even sympathy. It is a Christlike job. The difficulties will be greatest at the time of the peace. That is, at the very moment when we shall be realizing with particular clearness that by force of arms alone were we able to save our country, our ideals, and our lives, we shall be having to call on the caution and the imagination. History will certainly show that that was not fully possible. Human nature has not come that far. But yet it is what we must try to do, what we hope to have the opportunity to do, what for civilization's sake we ought to do, and what we have pledged ourselves only as little as possible to fail to do.

Index